© 2024 Brand-aid.co

Nathan Pernia
Zero to Hero Marketer: Basic Marketing for Non-Marketers

Published by: Brand-Aid.co
Text Design by: Nathan Pernia
Cover Design by: Nathan Pernia
Photography by: Natalie Pernia
ISBN-13: 979-8-9903494-0-7

ZERO TO HERO MARKETER

BASIC MARKETING GUIDE FOR NON-MARKETERS

NATHAN PERNIA

Dedication

To the joy of my life, my wife and two kids.

Contents

INTRODUCTION

Marketing. It's a word that makes many a small business owner break out in a cold sweat.

Visions of sleazy used-car salesman pitches and baffling acronyms like "PPC" and "SEO" come to mind. You just want to focus on making your awesome product or providing your top-notch service... not become a social media guru or data wizard.

Problem is, without some marketing savvy, even the most brilliant business idea is likely to languish in obscurity. Customers can't magically sense how much you could help them. You've got to get yourself out there!

Here's the thing: marketing doesn't have to be painful, expensive, or a total personality overhaul.

Think of it less like those aggressive pop-up ads that stalk you across the internet and more like making a new friend. You'd start by finding common interests, offering something helpful, and building trust over time, right? Marketing works the same way!

Bad News: There's no overnight millionaire magic bullet.

Good News: With the right foundation and a willingness to experiment, you CAN learn to attract your dream customers, build a loyal following, and grow your business in a way that feels authentic and, dare we say, even fun.

This guide is your marketing translator.

We'll demystify the jargon, break things down into bite-sized steps, and replace that sense of overwhelm with a can-do attitude.

Think of this book as your marketing-savvy friend who believes in your potential, even when you doubt yourself.

Spoiler Alert: You may realize you already possess the most important marketing skill – passion for what you do and a genuine desire to help others. We'll build on that!

Who This Book Is For:

- **Solopreneurs scrambling to wear ALL the hats:** We'll focus on what moves the needle, not vanity projects that eat up your time.

- **Small business owners on a shoestring budget:** Tons of effective marketing is low-cost or even free.

- **Folks who cringe at the idea of "selling out":** We'll focus on building relationships, not obnoxious hard sells.

- **Individuals trying to promote themselves:** We all have to do it at some point or another, whether trying to land a career or get someone's attention.

- **Seasoned marketers needing a refresher:** Yes, if you're a pro, this guide could help you too.

This Book Is for You If...

- You secretly believe marketing is important but feel lost and overwhelmed.

- You want to grow your business without sacrificing your integrity.

- You're ready to roll up your sleeves and learn some new skills that will pay off for years to come.

Get ready to transform your view of marketing. Think of it less as a chore and more as the key to connecting your amazing work with the people who need it most. Let's dive in!

The Importance of Marketing

"If you build it, they will come." Sadly, this only works in cheesy movies.

Imagine you've invented the world's most comfortable and stylish self-cleaning shoe (hey, we can dream!). But, if no one knows it exists, you're stuck with a garage full of unsold awesomeness. That's where marketing swoops in to save the day.

Think of marketing as your megaphone, your spotlight, and your invitation all rolled into one.

It's how you:

- **Get Discovered:** In a sea of competitors, marketing helps you cut through the noise and reach the right people.

- **Build Trust:** Nobody buys from strangers. Marketing gives you a chance to show your expertise, solve potential customers' problems, and prove why you're the best choice.

- **Turn Interest Into Action:** Maybe they like your stuff, but something's holding them back. Great marketing anticipates those objections and guides people towards saying YES to that purchase.

"But I hate sleazy sales tactics!"

Good news – you don't need them! Modern marketing is about relationships, not pushy pitches. Think of it like this:

- **Bad Marketing:** Shouting about your features from a mountaintop, hoping someone far below cares.

- **Good Marketing:** Having an engaging conversation at a party, discovering what someone needs, and naturally mentioning how you might be able to help.

Case Study: The Invisible Baker

Susan made the best cakes in town. Friends raved, but word-of-mouth only went so far. Then she took a few steps we'll cover in this book:

- **Niched Down:** Became THE source for gluten-free wedding cakes (less competition, passionate audience!).

- **Simple Website:** Showcase her creations, not tech-wizardry.

- **Targeted Instagram Posts:** Drool-worthy photos + partnering with local venues got booked solid.

Was it overnight success? Nope! But consistent, strategic marketing made her passion a profitable business.

Marketing Done Right Makes EVERYTHING Easier

When you get the word out effectively, you:

- **Attract Better Clients:** People who already 'get' what you do and are excited to pay.

- **Charge What You're Worth:** Confidence to ditch the bargain-basement pricing.

- **Waste Less Time:** No more random 'spray and pray' tactics that lead nowhere.

- **Enjoy the Process:** Marketing can (and should!) be aligned with your values.

Let's bust the myth that you need to be an extroverted, data-obsessed whiz kid to succeed at marketing. You just need the right road map, which is exactly what you'll find within these pages!

Misconceptions about Marketing

Let's Play MythBusters: Marketing Edition

When most people hear "marketing," certain images pop into their heads: slick Super Bowl ads, obnoxious pop-ups, and telemarketers interrupting dinner. Yuck! No wonder you might be tempted to skip this whole thing altogether.

But here's the deal: those annoyances are just the tip of the marketing iceberg, and often the worst examples of it done poorly. Great marketing is a lot subtler and way more powerful than flashy but shallow tactics.

Let's bust some common myths that might be holding you back:

Myth #1: Marketing = Advertising

Advertising (paid stuff like TV commercials or online ads) is just ONE piece of the marketing puzzle. Think of marketing as the big-picture strategy, while advertising is a tool you might use within that strategy.

Example: A local plumber fixing a leaky faucet for an elderly client and leaving a fridge magnet is marketing. So is their Google listing that pops up when someone searches "emergency plumber near me." One was free, one cost money... both are important.

Myth #2: You Need a Giant Budget

Sure, those splashy ad campaigns cost a fortune. But guess what? Plenty of scrappy businesses thrive with clever, low-budget marketing. Sometimes, creativity beats deep pockets!

Example: A food truck with no money for traditional advertising creates a hilarious TikTok series showcasing their unique menu items. They go viral, get tons of free publicity, and lines form around the block.

Myth #3: It's All About Being Fake & Pushy

Ugh, the slimy used-car salesman stereotype. Good news: nobody actually buys from people they don't trust! Authenticity and building genuine connections are at the heart of effective modern marketing.

Myth #4: Only Big Companies Need to "Do Marketing"

Whether you're a solo freelancer or a multinational corporation, marketing principles apply. The scale changes, but the goal is the same: reach the right people with the right message and turn them into loyal customers.

Myth #5: Marketing is All Fun & Games

Don't get me wrong, there are moments of "Hey, this is cool!" But it also takes work, analysis, and sometimes pivoting when things don't go to plan. Think less frivolous, more focused.

The Right Mindset Shift

Instead of seeing marketing as a manipulative chore, try this:

- **It's Problem-Solving:** What are your customers' pain points, and how does your business provide the solution?

- **It's Storytelling:** Share your passion in a compelling way that resonates.

- **It's Connection:** Build relationships based on trust, long before you ask for the sale.

This book will empower you to shed the misconceptions and embrace a view of marketing that feels authentic to you AND gets results for your business. Ready to dive in?

Can You Relate?

Meet Joe, King of the Kitchen Remodels

Joe and his small crew were the best in the business. Beautiful craftsmanship, meticulous attention to detail... every kitchen renovation they finished was magazine-worthy. Problem was, not enough people knew they existed.

Joe figured word-of-mouth would keep him booked solid. Sure, happy clients raved to their friends, but that was slow and unpredictable. Meanwhile, his slick-talking competitor with the flashy billboards seemed to be getting all the jobs, even though their reputation for shoddy work was whispered about in town.

This drove Joe nuts! He figured, "If people could just SEE the quality of what we do, they'd hire us in a heartbeat." But he was clueless when it came to anything beyond swinging a hammer. Terms like "content marketing" made his head hurt.

Joe wasn't lazy. He was exhausted after long days on job sites, and the idea of figuring out Facebook ads in the evenings was less appealing than having his teeth cleaned.

Sound Familiar?

Maybe you're not in construction, but you resonate with Joe's frustration. You have incredible skills – designing websites, providing therapy, baking delicious gluten-free treats. But the "business" side of things feels like a foreign language you never bothered to learn.

The fear is real: what if you're doomed to always be the best-kept secret, while less-talented competitors thrive simply because they're better at playing the marketing game?

It doesn't have to be this way! Imagine if Joe...

- Snapped simple before-and-after photos of his projects, showcasing his work on Instagram instead of dusty old brochures.

- Partnered with local realtors, offering move-in-ready kitchen updates to boost property values.

- Started a no-pressure email newsletter with home improvement tips, building trust long before anyone needed a full remodel.

None of this requires Joe to become a social media influencer or hire a fancy ad agency. It's about making his amazing work visible to the RIGHT audience, in a way that feels true to who he is.

This book is your road map to a similar transformation. We'll break down the intimidating marketing concepts into manageable steps and empower you to take action without sacrificing your integrity (or your sanity!).

Let's turn that "nobody knows I exist" feeling into a steady stream of your dream customers excited to work with you. Your skills deserve to be seen!

Marketing isn't complex magic; it's learnable skills that anyone can apply.

Spoiler Alert: You're Already a Marketer, You Just Don't Know It Yet

Think back to when you were a kid, desperately wanting that new toy. How'd you convince your parents? Maybe you:

- Demonstrated how it worked and why it was SO much better than your old stuff.

- Negotiated by offering to do extra chores in exchange.

- Subtly dropped hints for weeks, hoping they'd take pity on you.

Guess what? That was marketing! Sure, the stakes were lower than growing your business, but the core principles are the same.

See, marketing isn't some dark magic practiced only by those fluent in analytics and acronyms. It's about understanding what people want, communicating your value clearly, and building a little bit of "gotta have it" desire.

The Problem with "Marketing Gurus"

They make it look easy. Launch a quick webinar, run a few ads, and BOOM! Money rains from the sky while they sip margaritas on a beach. Reality is rarely that simple. Those folks often have teams and years of experience we don't see behind the curtain.

Trying to replicate their overnight success stories can be discouraging. It's like watching an Olympic gymnast and then beating yourself up for not being able to do a perfect backflip on your first try.

The Good News: Marketing IS Learnable

Just like you wouldn't expect to become a skilled baker without a recipe and some practice, you need a good guide and the willingness to experiment to get results with marketing. Think of it like this:

- **Marketing Strategy is Your Recipe:** It provides the ingredients (different tactics) and the process for combining them for the desired outcome.

- **Data is Your Taste-Testing:** Did that cake turn out moist and delicious, or dry and crumbly? Data tells you what's working and what needs tweaking.

- **Consistency is Key:** Even the best pastry chefs have flops sometimes. The key is to keep baking (and learning!).

Case Study: The Accidental Marketer

John owned a small hardware store. He thought marketing was pointless – his customers were mostly older folks resistant to change. Then, he started...

- Posting funny TikTok videos explaining how to fix common household problems.

- Partnering with a local influencer to showcase how his products could be used in DIY projects.

- Sending a simple email reminder to customers when it was time to replace their furnace filters.

Surprise! Turns out people DID appreciate his knowledge and humor. New customers discovered him, existing ones bought more often... all from taking a few simple (and fun!) marketing actions.

Why this Book?

Here's What's Different About This Guide

- **No Jargon Jungle:** We'll define those buzzwords in plain English, no business degree required.

- **Action > Theory:** Every concept is paired with practical steps you can take TODAY, even if you only have 15 minutes to spare.

- **Built on Empathy:** It all starts with understanding your ideal customer, NOT copying what big brands do with their giant budgets.

This book isn't a magic wand, but it's the next best thing.

It's a road map, a toolbox, and a much-needed pep talk to help you unlock your marketing potential and grow your business with confidence. Let's do this!

This book will demystify the process.

We'll break down the essentials into bite-sized pieces, ditch the jargon, and focus on what TRULY moves the needle for YOUR business. You may not become a marketing wizard overnight, but you will gain the clarity and confidence to make informed decisions, see what works, and ditch what doesn't.

Let's turn that "I'm terrible at marketing" feeling into "Hey, I'm getting the hang of this!"

PART I:

MARKETING FOUNDATIONS

CHAPTER 1:

DEFINING YOUR IDEAL CUSTOMER

"Imagine knowing your perfect customer so well, it's like you can read their mind. That's the power of understanding your target audience..."

Understanding Demographics and Psychographics

Unlocking the Secret Code: Understanding Demographics and Psychographics

Imagine you're at a crowded party, trying to find your best friend. You could shout their name, but that would attract a lot of confused stares. A smarter approach? Knowing what they look like (the obvious stuff) and their usual hangout spots (the deeper interests). Marketing is surprisingly similar – you need to know who you're looking for to find them effectively. That's where demographics and psychographics come in!

Demographics: The "What" of Your Customer

Demographics are the easy-to-spot details about your ideal customer. Think of them like a person's ID card:

- **Age:** Are you targeting college students or retirees? The products they need and how you reach them will be wildly different.

- **Location:** A local bakery and an online clothing store have different geographical focuses.

- **Income:** This impacts what people can afford. Luxury brands have a different audience than bargain-focused ones.

- **Gender:** While we must avoid outdated stereotypes, some products or services naturally appeal more to particular genders.

- **Family Situation:** Single folks vs. parents with young kids have vastly different shopping priorities.

Psychographics: The "Why" of Your Customer

Psychographics delve into the mind of your customer. It's less about what they are, and more about how they think. This includes:

- **Personality:** Are they introverted or extroverted? Practical or impulsive? This impacts how you word your marketing messages.

- **Values:** Do they prioritize sustainability, status, or convenience? This should be reflected in your brand messaging.

- **Interests:** An outdoorsy person is more likely to respond to gear ads than a fashionista, even if they're the same age and income level.

- **Lifestyles:** Think busy professional vs. stay-at-home parent. Their daily routines affect when and how they shop.

- **Pain Points:** What problems do they desperately want to solve? Your product or service should feel like the perfect answer.

Case Study: Sneakers That Aren't Just About Running

Let's say you're selling high-tech running shoes. Here's how demographics and psychographics create different customer profiles:

- **Customer 1:** Sarah, 32, urban professional, decent income. She's into fitness but also cares about style. She wants shoes for gym workouts and to look good athleisure-style with jeans.

- **Customer 2:** Bob, 55, suburban dad, health conscious. He's less about fashion but prioritizes comfort and joint support due to old sports injuries.

See the difference? Even though both might search "running shoes," their needs and what will get them excited are vastly different.

Why Bother with All This?

Knowing your ideal customer inside-out has massive benefits:

- **Laser-focused Marketing:** Imagine trying to sell baby supplies to college students – waste of time! Demographics and psychographics keep you on target.

- **Speak Their Language:** A yoga studio targeting stressed-out executives will have different messaging than one aimed at bendy college kids.

- **Find Them Where They Hang Out:** Should you spend time on TikTok or prioritize industry magazines? Your ideal customer's hangouts give you clues.

Warning: Beware of Assumptions!

"All women love chocolate!" or "Retirees don't use social media!" are lazy stereotypes. Always back up your assumptions about your customers with data. This can be:

- **Surveys:** Ask existing customers or a target group to fill out questionnaires.

- **Social Media Insights:** Platforms offer analytics on who interacts with your content.

- **Market Research:** See if existing studies match your hunch about your audience.

The Marketing Superhero Power

Understanding demographics and psychographics is like having customer-finding X-ray vision. You won't waste time on the wrong people, and your marketing will hit the sweet spot every time. Ready to unlock this power?

Creating Customer Personas/ Avatars

Meet Your New Best Friends: Crafting Customer Personas

Imagine having a few friends who embody everything about your perfect customer. You know their favorite foods, their pet peeves, and exactly what makes them tick. Wouldn't marketing be a breeze? That's the magic of customer personas (also called avatars)!

What the Heck is a Persona?

A customer persona is a fictional character that represents a segment of your ideal audience. It's not just jotting down some demographics; it's giving them a name, a face, and a backstory richer than a soap opera character!

Why You Need Personas in Your Life

- **Stop Talking to Yourself:** Ever written marketing copy and wondered, "Will anyone actually find this interesting?" Personas keep you focused on your customer, not your own opinions.

- **Make Decisions Easier:** "Should we make our blog posts funny or serious?" Boom! Check your persona. Is 'Serious Sally' likely to appreciate your meme collection? Probably not.

- **Humanize Your Marketing:** It's easy to see customers as numbers. Personas remind you there's a real person with hopes, fears, and maybe a weird obsession with cat videos on the other side of that purchase.

Building Your Persona Squad

Let's make this fun! Think of it like creating characters for a book:

- **The Basics:** Start with the demographics and psychographics we discussed earlier. Give your persona a name (alliteration is fun – Marketing Mike, Tech-Savvy Tina). Stock photos can help visualize them!

- **Dig Deeper:** Imagine their day-to-day life:

  » **Job/Role:** What do they do? What stresses them out at work?

  » **Goals:** What do they dream about? Bigger house, less hectic schedule, the perfect pair of sneakers...

» **Challenges:** What obstacles keep them from those goals? Tight budget, lack of time, finding reliable information...

» **Online Habits:** What social platforms are their guilty pleasure? Do they read blogs or prefer podcasts?

- **Get Specific (and a Little Weird):**

  » **Favorite Brands:** Tells you what kind of quality and image they value.

  » **Biggest Fears:** Worried about product scams, looking foolish – this impacts how you reassure them.

  » **Quirks:** Do they adore sloths? Hate the sound of chewing? Odd details make your persona feel more real.

Case Study: The Coffee Shop Persona Clash

Let's say you own a coffee shop. Here are two potential personas:

- **Frantic Fran:** College student, always on the go, fueled by caffeine and dreams of good grades. She needs fast service, budget-friendly options, and maybe a loyalty program for all those late-night study sessions.

- **Chill Chad:** Works remotely, tired of his home office. Wants comfy seating, reliable Wi-Fi, and premium coffee to justify the higher price than his kitchen drip machine.

See how different ads, promotions, and even your shop's décor would change to cater to either Fran or Chad?

Don't Go Overboard

Start with 2-3 well-defined personas. You can always add more later. Too many and it gets overwhelming!

Where to Get Your Info

- **Mine Your Data:** Look at your customer base. Any patterns in age, location, what they buy?

- **Interview Real People:** Loyal customers are usually happy to chat in exchange for a free coffee!

- **Competitor Recon:** See who THEY seem to be targeting (but do it better, of course!).

Keep Your Personas Alive

Don't stick these in a drawer! Refer to them when writing website copy, designing ads, or choosing what new product to develop. Would 'Practical Paula' be excited about it? If not, back to the drawing board!

Personas are your marketing superpower. Building them is fun, but more importantly, they help you get results by keeping your ideal customer close to your heart.

CHAPTER 2:

YOUR VALUE PROPOSITION

"In a sea of similar options, what makes you the special catch? Let's craft a value proposition that makes customers say, 'I need that!'"

What Makes You Unique and Different from Competitors?

Stand Out or Fade Out: Crafting Your Unique Value Proposition (UVP)

In a world overflowing with options, why should a customer choose YOU? That's the million-dollar question answered by your value proposition. It's the promise you make and the reason someone picks your business over a dozen nearly identical ones. Let's make yours so good, it'd be crazy to go anywhere else!

Warning: "We Have Great Service" Isn't Enough

Every business owner on the planet thinks they offer quality products and stellar service. Those are important, of course, but they're not what sets you apart. We need to dig deeper!

Step 1: Know Thine Enemy (AKA Your Competition)

Don't be that blissfully unaware business owner who claims, " I have no competitors!" Everyone does.

- **Direct Competitors:** Businesses selling the same or very similar products/services as you.

- **Indirect Competitors:** Businesses who fulfill the same need but in a different way. A takeout pizza joint competes with cozy restaurants AND the grocery store's frozen aisle.

Time for some detective work:

- **Scour Their Websites:** How do they describe themselves? What do they emphasize?

- **Check Customer Reviews:** What do people rave about (and complain about!)? This gives you clues to their strengths and potential weaknesses.

- **Mystery Shop (If Possible):** Experience them as a customer would. Notice anything that makes them stand out or stumble.

Step 2: Turn the Spotlight on Yourself

Now it's time for some soul-searching. Ask yourself these questions (and be brutally honest!):

- **What Do You Do Best?** Maybe you have the fastest turnaround time, the most customizable options, or expertise nobody else in town offers.

- **What's Your 'Special Sauce'?** Is it a family recipe, a unique process, or a personality-driven brand that's impossible to replicate?

- **Why Do Customers Love You?** Look at testimonials, ask loyal customers directly... heck, if someone complimented your stellar parking lot, note even the oddball stuff!

Step 3: Find the Sweet Spot

This is where the magic happens! You're looking for the overlap between:

- What you do uniquely well

- What your ideal customer desperately needs

- Where your competitors fall short

Case Study: The Dog Walker With a Difference

Let's say you're in a town with lots of dog walkers. Here's how to stand out:

- **Competitors:** Basic walks, maybe some playtime. Focus is on pet owners without time.

- **Your Superpower:** You're a certified dog trainer. You offer exercise AND help with behavioral issues like leash pulling or anxiety.

- **Perfect Customer:** Owners of "problem pups" and those who want the absolute best for their furry friend.

- **Value Prop Example:** "Transform your walks from stressful to joyful – expert dog walker and trainer helps even the most challenging dogs become perfect walking buddies!"

See how that beats the generic "I love dogs, will walk them"?

Value Proposition Power-Ups

Here's how to strengthen your statement:

- **Be Specific:** Ditch vague words like "quality" or "exceptional." Quantifiable wins - do you respond to inquiries faster than anyone else? State it!

- **Focus on Benefits, Not Features:** Customers care about what your product/service DOES for them. "Hand-crafted soap" is a feature. "Soothing your sensitive skin with natural ingredients" is the benefit that makes them reach for their wallet.

- **Keep it Short and Sweet:** Nobody reads essay-length value propositions. Aim for a single, memorable sentence.

A Word on Pricing

Being the cheapest is rarely a sustainable strategy (hello, race to the bottom!). If you can justify charging more due to your unique value, do it! Don't compete on price, compete on being so awesome it's a no-brainer.

The Ever-Evolving Value Proposition

Your business grows and changes. Revisit your value proposition every so often. Does it still align with what you offer and what your customers want? Don't be afraid to tweak it!

Why Should Someone Choose You?

From "Meh" to "Must-Have": Answering the Customer's Burning Question

Imagine walking down a supermarket aisle packed with near-identical brands of cereal. What makes you grab the brightly colored box with the cartoon mascot over the boring-looking one? That, my friend, is the power of answering the question, "Why should someone choose you?"

It's Not About You, It's About Them

Here's the biggest mistake businesses make: they focus on how awesome THEY are. Fastest shipping! Award-winning team! Blah, blah, blah. Customers are a selfish bunch (and rightfully so!). They care about one thing: what's in it for them?

Your job is to connect the dots: Here's your problem, and here's how I solve it better than anyone else.

Let's Break This Down

To answer the "why you?" question convincingly, focus on these three areas:

- **The Problem You Solve:**

  » Does your product make life easier, save time, or relieve stress?

  » Do you offer entertainment, a sense of community, or a boost of confidence?

  » Be specific! "We help people relax" is weak. "We help overwhelmed working moms carve out guilt-free 'me-time'" is far more powerful.

- **The Results You Deliver:**

  » Don't just tell me your skincare is "nourishing," tell me I'll have fewer wrinkles and a radiant glow!

  » Quantifiable results are best: "Lose 5 pounds in a month!" "Get 10 more hours of sleep a week!"

» Emotional results matter too: "Feel confident walking into any room," "Impress your boss with your newfound knowledge."

- **What Makes You Special:**

  » This is where your value proposition (which we covered earlier) shines.

  » It's the combo of what you offer + how it's uniquely tailored to your ideal customer's needs.

Case Study: The Freelance Writer Wars

Tons of freelancers claim to write great content. Here's how to stand out:

- **Boring Approach:** "I write SEO-friendly articles and blog posts!" Yawn. So does everyone else.

- **"Why You" Power Approach:** "I specialize in helping wellness brands turn complex health topics into engaging, reader-friendly blog posts that boost their credibility and search rankings."

See the difference? The second one screams, "If you're in the wellness space and struggle to explain things in plain English, I'm your solution!"

Proof is in the Pudding

Nobody believes claims without evidence. Here's how to back up your "why you" statement:

- **Testimonials/Reviews:** Glowing words from happy customers are marketing gold.

- **Case Studies:** "Before using our service, Client X struggled with... after, they saw [amazing results]."

- **Data/Stats:** "Our cleaning products eliminate 99.9% of germs" is more compelling than just "super clean."

- **Social Proof:** "Trusted by 10,000+ businesses" builds instant credibility.

A Note on "Guarantees"

Love them or hate them, a strong guarantee can be a difference-maker. "Love your new haircut, or your money back!" removes the risk for a hesitant customer. But make sure you can actually deliver on that promise!

The Final Test

Read your "why you" statement. Does it:

- Immediately make sense to your ideal customer?

- Focus on THEM and the results you deliver?

- Make you want to do business with yourself?

If not, it's time for a rewrite!

This exercise is tough but transformative. Once you can clearly articulate why someone should choose you, selling becomes a whole lot easier!

CHAPTER 3:

BRANDING BASICS

"Your brand is more than just a logo. It's the personality of your business. Let's make yours unforgettable."

Developing a Memorable Name, Logo, and Brand Voice

Branding 101: Making Your Business Unforgettable

Think of the world's most famous brands – Apple, Nike, Disney. Their names, logos, and unique vibes are instantly recognizable. That's the power of great branding! It's not about being the biggest company; it's about carving a space in your customer's mind. Let's get started!

Part 1: Choose a Name That Sticks

Your business name is its first impression. Here's what makes a great one:

- **Easy to Say and Spell:** If people stumble over pronouncing it or constantly get the spelling wrong, it's a marketing nightmare.

- **Memorable:** "Bob's Accounting Services" is forgettable. "Tax Terminator" is... well, not forgettable (though maybe too cheesy!).

- **Relevant:** Cute names are fun, but if it has zero connection to what you do, it's confusing. A bakery named "Whiskers & Paws" brings to mind pet supplies, not yummy cupcakes.

- **Available:** Do your homework! Ensure the name (and matching web domain) isn't already taken.

Name Brainstorming Tips:

- **Play with Words:** Puns, alliteration ("Dunkin' Donuts"), or unexpected combinations can be catchy.

- **Use Your Unique Value Proposition (UVP):** Got a unique ingredient or process? Weave it into the name.

- **The Founder's Flair:** Works if your name is distinctive (think "Ben & Jerry's"). Less so if your name is super common.

Part 2: Design a Logo That Pops

Your logo isn't just decoration, it represents your brand at a glance. Keep it:

- **Simple:** Too busy, and it's unmemorable. Think of Apple's iconic... apple.

- **Scalable:** Needs to look good on a giant billboard AND a tiny social media icon.

- **Timeless:** Avoid trendy fonts or colors that will look dated quickly.

- **Reflects Your Brand:** A playful, colorful logo fits a kids' toy store, not so much a serious law firm.

DIY or Hire a Pro?

If you're on a tight budget, online logo makers are a starting point. **BUT** a professional designer can bring a level of strategy and polish you won't get from a template.

Part 3: Find Your Brand Voice

How would your brand speak if it were a person? This is essential for making all your marketing feel consistent. Consider:

- **Formal vs. Casual:** Law firm? Better be professional. Surfing gear shop? Relaxed vibes allowed.

- **Humorous vs. Serious:** Does your brand make people laugh, or should it be strictly no-nonsense?

- **Vocabulary:** Complicated jargon or easy-to-understand language? Match your audience!

Case Study: The Rebranded Coffee Shop

Linda's coffee shop was called "The Daily Grind." Blah name, generic logo, and its social media posts were filled with coffee memes, failing to stand out. Rebranding time!

- **New Name:** "The Cozy Cup" – Inviting image of warmth and relaxation.

- **Logo:** Simple illustration of a steaming mug with a comfy armchair tucked into the curve.

- **Brand Voice:** Friendly and welcoming, like your favorite barista. Tips on brewing better coffee at home, not just "buy our beans!"

The result? The place feels more cohesive, attracts its ideal customers (people seeking a chill hangout, not just a caffeine jolt), and Linda's marketing is way more effective now!

Brand Voice Exercise

List 3-5 adjectives that describe your ideal brand personality. Now, practice writing a few things from your brand's point of view:

- A website "About Us" blurb

-

- A social media post promoting a sale

- An email responding to a customer question

Does it sound consistent? If not, you need more refining!

Warning: Don't Copy the Big Guys

It's tempting to mimic successful brands. But what works for a giant corporation won't for a small, local biz. Being authentically YOU is what attracts your perfect customers.

Your Brand is an Evolution

Start with these basics, and as your business grows, so can your branding. Revisit it periodically to ensure it still matches your vibe and attracts your dream audience.

Consistency in Messaging

Why Consistent Messaging is Your Branding Superpower

Imagine your business is a person attending a huge party. Consistent messaging is like them wearing a recognizable outfit and introducing themselves the same way to everyone they meet. Inconsistent messaging is like them changing clothes every five minutes, yelling out a different name, and confusing the heck out of everyone!

What Consistency IS... and ISN'T

- **Consistency IS:**
    - » Using the same logo, colors, and fonts everywhere.
    - » Your brand voice sounding similar across your website, emails, and in-person chats.
    - » Your core values shining through in all your actions.

- **Consistency ISN'T:**
    - » Saying the EXACT same thing, word for word, on every platform. That's boring!
    - » Never experimenting or adjusting your message as you learn about your audience.
    - » Being afraid to have a little fun and shake things up occasionally.

Why Bother Being Consistent?

- **Builds Recognition and Trust:** Think of McDonald's golden arches. You know what kind of food and experience to expect anywhere in the world. That's powerful!

- **Makes You Memorable:** Sporadic marketing with mixed messages is easily forgotten. Consistency helps you stick in your customers' minds.

- **Looks Professional:** If your website is sleek, but your social media feels like it's run by a meme-obsessed teen, that's jarring! Consistency makes you look polished and put together.

- **Saves Time (and Sanity):** Not having to reinvent the wheel for every email or blog post frees up your brainpower for better things.

Case Study: The Hot Mess vs. The Polished Pro

- **Business #1:** Their website is sleek, focusing on luxury services. Their Instagram is full of grainy selfies and rants about difficult clients. Yikes! This makes me question their professionalism.

- **Business #2:** Their branding is bright, friendly, and focused on affordability. This carries over in their social media captions full of money-saving tips, and their customer service is as cheery as their logo. This feels cohesive and trustworthy!

How to Achieve Consistency

- **Brand Guidelines:** This simple document states your official:

- » Logo variations and how to use them

- » Color palette (with exact color codes!)

- » Fonts

- » Brand voice examples (see the last section!)

- **Templates:** Create templates for things you use frequently:

  - » Social media graphics

  - » Email newsletters

  - » Slide decks

- **Do an Audit:** Gather EVERYTHING customer-facing. Does it give a cohesive impression? If not, it's time for a makeover!

Balancing Consistency with Flexibility

Different platforms have different vibes. Here's how to adjust your message while staying "on-brand":

- **LinkedIn vs. TikTok:** Professional network vs. fun short videos. Your core message is the same (what you do, who you help), but the TONE shifts.

- **Responding to Comments:** Stay true to your voice, but a cranky customer calls for empathy, while a gushing fan warrants matching their enthusiasm.

- **Big Sales vs. Everyday Content:** It's okay to get a bit louder and more sales-y during a promotion, as long as it's not wildly out of character for your brand.

Beware of Schizophrenic Branding

This happens as businesses grow:

- The founder's original vision gets muddled as more people get involved.

- Marketing agencies are hired without understanding the core brand.

- Trendy slogans and visuals get thrown in randomly because "that's what everyone else does."

Regular check-ins are key! Does a new campaign or piece of content FEEL like your brand? If not, back to the drawing board.

Consistency takes effort, but the payoff is huge. Your marketing becomes more effective, your business becomes unforgettable, and customers begin to trust you even before they buy!

PART II:

ESSENTIAL MARKETING CHANNELS

CHAPTER 4:

THE MARKETING FUNNEL

"Think of your marketing like a friendly guide. In this chapter, we'll design the path that takes a stranger and turns them into a loyal customer."

Awareness, Interest, Consideration, Decision, Action

The Marketing Funnel: Your Customer's Journey Made Simple

Think of finding true love (or at least a decent date). You don't walk up to a stranger and immediately propose marriage! There are stages – noticing them, getting curious, first date, and hopefully, a happily-ever-after. Marketing works the same way.

That's where the marketing funnel comes in. It's a way to visualize the steps someone takes from "Who the heck are you?" to "I love this company!" Your job is to guide them along that path.

Let's Break it Down

Here's a simplified version of the classic marketing funnel:

- **Awareness:** This is where people first discover you exist. Think of it like spotting someone cute across a crowded room.

- **Interest:** They're intrigued! "Hmm, they seem interesting, maybe I'll learn more." This is the flirting stage.

- **Consideration:** Things are getting serious. They're comparing you to other options (aka your competition!). This is like weighing the pros and cons before making a move.

- **Decision:** It's commitment time! They choose to buy your product, sign up for your service, etc. It's the relationship equivalent of saying "They're the one."

- **Action:** They actually take the desired action, whether it's a purchase or something else. In the dating world, this is the first kiss (or at least exchanging numbers!).

Case Study: Luring in a Coffee Lover

Let's say you own a coffee shop. Here's how the funnel might work:

- **Awareness:** Ads on Instagram featuring mouthwatering latte art, or a funny sign outside your shop catches their eye.

- **Interest:** They check your website – cool atmosphere, unique menu items...worth exploring!

- **Consideration:** They compare your prices to Starbucks, read online reviews, maybe scope your location on a map.

- **Decision:** The craving wins! They decide to ditch their usual chain coffee and give you a try.

- **Action:** They walk in the door and order that tempting-looking drink.

Why Does the Funnel Shape Matter?

It illustrates that you'll have TONS of people at the awareness stage (everyone who glances at your ad), but only a fraction will become paying customers. That's normal! Focus on moving people down the funnel, not getting everyone to buy immediately.

Your Strategy Changes at Each Stage

- Top of Funnel (Awareness):

- » **Goal:** Get noticed!

- » **Tactics:** Eye-catching social posts, search engine ads, PR stunts (think giant inflatable mascot, but tastefully done!)

- Middle of Funnel (Interest/Consideration):

  - » **Goal:** Build trust and highlight what sets you apart.

  - » **Tactics:** Email newsletters with valuable tips, webinars, comparison guides, glowing testimonials

- Bottom of Funnel (Decision/Action):

  - » **Goal:** Seal the deal!

  - » **Tactics:** Limited-time offers, free trials, abandoned cart emails (reminding shoppers what they left behind)

Funnels Get Messy in Real Life

Customers don't always follow this neatly. They might bounce around stages or get stuck for a while. A customer on your email list might suddenly click a Facebook ad and finally buy. That's why being present on multiple channels is essential!

The Sneaky Post-Funnel Stage

You got the sale, congrats! But the funnel's not over! Don't forget about:

- **Retention:** Keeping customers happy so they buy again and become loyal fans.

- **Advocacy:** Turning them into raving reviewers and getting them to recommend you to others, which brings in new leads at the top of YOUR funnel.

The marketing funnel is one of the most fundamental concepts to grasp. Understanding where your potential customers are in their journey means delivering the right kind of marketing at the right time. It's the difference between annoying people with irrelevant sales pitches and becoming their trusted go-to solution!

How to Guide Potential Customers Through the Journey

Become a Marketing Tour Guide: Leading Customers Down the Funnel

Remember, the marketing funnel is about the customer's journey, not yours. You can't force someone to instantly fall in love with your brand. But, with thoughtful strategy, you can be their helpful (and not annoyingly pushy) guide.

Mapping Out the Ideal Trip

Start by envisioning the perfect path someone might take to become a loyal customer. This will be different for every business. Here are some questions to ponder:

- **Where do they hang out?** Which social platforms, websites, or even real-world places does your ideal customer frequent?

- **What are their pain points?** What problems do they need solved that your product or service addresses?

- **What objections might they have?** Is price a major concern? Do they worry your solution won't work?

Example: Skincare Buyer's Journey

Let's say you sell natural skincare for sensitive skin. Your customer journey might look something like this:

- **Awareness:** Instagram ads featuring soothing imagery or articles on blogs about managing sensitive skin.

- **Interest:** Visiting your website, drawn in by informative content and before/after photos.

- **Consideration:** Reading product reviews, comparing ingredients, maybe signing up for emails for a discount code.

- **Decision:** Taking the plunge on a small "sample size" or introductory set.

- **Action:** They love the results and purchase full-size versions.

Smoothing Out the Road

Now, think about potential bumps at each stage:

- **Awareness:** Are your ads getting seen by the right audience?

- **Interest:** Is your website ugly, confusing, or slow to load? Bye-bye, potential customer!

- **Consideration:** Lack of reviews, pushy sales tactics, or a complicated checkout process can all lead to lost sales.

Your job is to remove those obstacles and make the journey as enjoyable as possible!

Tools for Each Stage of the Funnel

Let's get practical. Here are some common tactics and how they map to the funnel:

- Top of Funnel (Awareness):

  » **Social Media Ads:** Highly targeted to reach your ideal customers.

  » **Blog Posts Optimized for Search (SEO):** Help people with relevant questions find you organically.

  » **Influencer Partnerships:** Tap into existing audiences that trust certain personalities.

- Middle of Funnel (Interest/Consideration):

  » **Email Marketing:** Stay in touch with potential customers with a regular newsletter.

  » **Case Studies/Testimonials:** Proving your product works builds confidence.

  » **Webinars/Free Workshops:** Share expertise and position yourself as an authority.

- Bottom of Funnel (Decision/Action):

- » **Sales Pages:** Clear, persuasive copy that addresses common objections and makes buying easy.

- » **Limited-Time Offers/Discounts:** Creates a sense of urgency.

- » **Retargeting Ads:** Remind people who visited your website about that product still in their cart.

The Art of the Nudge (Not the Nag)

Nobody likes a desperate salesperson. Guide your customers along with:

- Helpful Content: Answer their questions, even if it doesn't scream "buy my stuff!" immediately.

- Building Relationships: Be responsive on social media, personalize emails when possible.

- Adding Value at Every Stage: Even those who don't buy should find your interaction beneficial.

Case Study: The Non-Spammy Email Campaign

A photographer could offer a downloadable guide to "Preparing for Your Family Photoshoot" when people sign up for their email list. This provides value, AND when it's time to book photos, guess who'll be top of mind?

The Long Game

Some people zoom through the funnel, others take their time. Don't lose hope if they don't buy right away. Consistent, valuable presence on various channels increases the odds they'll move forward when ready.

Remember, guiding customers through their journey is about building trust and offering solutions. It might take some time, but helping someone on their path to finding your amazing product or service is how you create raving fans for life!

CHAPTER 5:

BUILDING A WEBSITE THAT CONVERTS

"Your website is your online storefront. Let's make it not just pretty, but a place where visitors turn into customers."

Design, User Experience, and Content Basics

Your Website: The Digital Storefront That Works 24/7

Imagine your website is a physical store. A messy layout, broken links, and paragraphs of boring text are the equivalent of flickering lights, boxes blocking the aisles, and a bored salesclerk ignoring customers. Ouch! Let's make your website a welcoming place people want to spend time (and money!).

Design: It's Not Just About Being Pretty

Yes, your website should be visually appealing. But good design is about more than fancy fonts:

- **Easy Navigation:** Can visitors find what they need within a few clicks? A confusing menu leads to frustration and lost sales.

- **Visual Hierarchy:** Your most important info should stand out! Don't make people hunt for your contact details or special offers.

- **Mobile-First:** More people browse on phones than on computers. If your site looks wonky on small screens, say goodbye to potential customers.

- **Branding Consistency:** Match your website's look and feel to the rest of your branding – it reassures visitors they're in the right place.

Case Study: Death by Boring Design

- **Business:** Law firm specializing in complex business disputes.

  - » **Bad Website:** A giant wall of text in tiny font, gray background, no images. Makes me feel overwhelmed before I even read anything!

- **The Fix:** Clean layout, clear headings ("Do you need help with X?"), and visuals like graphs or simple icons to break up the text.

User Experience (UX): Make It a Pleasure, Not a Chore

Think of UX as how your website makes the visitor FEEL. Here's what matters:

- **Speed:** Every second of load time counts. People are impatient! Optimize images and ditch unnecessary bells and whistles that slow things down.

- **Simple Forms:** Asking for a ton of info upfront chases people away. Keep forms short and sweet, only gather essential details.

- **Clear Calls to Action:** "Learn More," "Buy Now," "Get a Quote"... tell visitors exactly what you want them to do on each page.

- **Error Handling:** "404 Page Not Found" is a dead end. A playful custom error page with search or links back to your main site saves the day.

Content: The Words That Sell (and Help You Get Found)

Design and UX get people in the door. Content is what makes them stay and eventually buy.

- **Focus on Your Customer:** Use language they understand. Less about your awards, more about how you solve their problems.

- **SEO Basics:** Keywords (what people search for) sprinkled naturally in your text help search engines like Google know what your site's about.

- **Not Just Text:** Break up giant paragraphs with images, videos, infographics... more visually engaging = people stick around longer.

- **Tell a Story:** Even "boring" industries can captivate! Testimonials and case studies add a human element compared to dry product descriptions.

Warning: DIY vs. Hiring a Pro

Website builders make it tempting to go it alone. But consider this:

- **Your Time is Valuable:** Struggling with a template can take forever. Is that the best use of your skills as a business owner?

- **First Impressions Matter:** A polished website screams professionalism, a clunky one damages trust before they even read your content.

- **Pros Know the Tech:** SEO, accessibility optimization, and things you haven't even heard of... a web designer ensures your site isn't just pretty but WORKS.

Website Checkup Time

Pretend you're a first-time visitor to your site:

- Can you immediately figure out what the business does and who it's for?

- Is finding important stuff like your services or "About" page easy?

- Do you feel compelled to click around and learn more... or run away screaming?

Don't be afraid of a website revamp if what you have isn't working. Think of it as an investment in getting more leads and sales. Your amazing website can be your top salesperson, even when you're asleep!

Introduction to Search Engine Optimization (SEO)

SEO: Your Website's Ticket to the Google Spotlight

Imagine you've opened the world's most incredible bakery. The cupcakes are mind-blowing, the decor is adorable, but... it's hidden down a dark alley. Unless someone stumbles upon it by accident, you're going to have a lot of stale pastries.

That's your website without SEO (Search Engine Optimization). It might be amazing, but if search engines like Google can't find it and understand what it's about, how will potential customers?

Speaking Google's Language

SEO is the art of making your website attractive to search engines. It's NOT about tricking Google with shady tactics. It's about giving clear signals that help them match your site with the right searches.

Think of Google as a giant librarian organizing the ENTIRE internet. Your website is one book in that massive library. SEO helps you put the right keywords on the cover, spine, and inside the book, so when someone searches "best cupcakes in [your city]," your bakery pops up!

The Two Flavors of SEO

- **On-Page SEO:** This is all about what you control on your own website:

  » **Keywords:** The words and phrases people search for. Tools like Google Keyword Planner (it's free!) help you find relevant ones.

  » **Title Tags and Descriptions:** The bits that show on search result pages – make them enticing and include your keywords.

  » **Clear Content Structure:** Headings, subheadings, and organized paragraphs make your content easy for Google (and humans) to digest.

- **Off-Page SEO:** This is about building your "reputation" around the web:

  » **Backlinks:** When other websites link to yours, it signals to Google that you're an authority. Guest blogging or getting featured by relevant sites can help.

  » **Social Signals:** While not a direct ranking factor, being active on social media can drive traffic to your site, which Google notices.

Case Study: The Invisible Yoga Studio

- **Problem:** A yoga studio's website was buried on page 5 of Google results for "yoga [their town]." Potential clients never found them!

- **SEO Fixes:**

  » Optimized their page titles to include "Yoga [Town Name] – Relaxing Classes for All Levels"

  » Added local keywords throughout their content ("Best yoga studio in [town name]")

  » Built backlinks by partnering with local businesses for cross-promotion

- **Result:** They moved to the top of Google results and saw a huge boost in website traffic and class sign-ups.

SEO Is an Ongoing Process

Don't expect to sprinkle some keyword magic and instantly rank #1. Here's why:

- **It Takes Time:** Google doesn't update its search results overnight. It can take weeks or even months to see significant movement.

- **The Competition Isn't Sleeping:** Other businesses are also doing SEO! This is a long-term game.

- **Google Changes the Rules:** Algorithms get updated, so what worked perfectly a year ago might not be as effective today.

Quick SEO Wins for Beginners

- **Target Local Searches:** "Plumber near me" is easier to rank for than just "plumber."

- **Nail Your Basics:** Great content relevant to your audience is more important than fancy tricks.

- **Focus on User Experience:** Google rewards websites people love to spend time on.

- **Use SEO Tools:** Free options like Google Analytics and Google Search Console give invaluable insights into how people are finding you.

Beware of Shady Shortcuts

Buying backlinks or keyword stuffing (cramming keywords in unnaturally) did work... back in 1998. Now it gets you penalized by Google. Slow and steady wins the SEO race!

Think of SEO as a Long-Term Investment

Done right, it keeps paying off in the form of:

- **More Organic Traffic:** People finding you without paid ads = lower marketing costs.

- **Higher Quality Leads:** They're searching for exactly what you offer, so they're more likely to convert to customers.

- **Increased Authority:** Ranking well makes you look like the expert in your space.

If the technical side of SEO makes your head spin, there are agencies and consultants specializing in this. Educate yourself on the basics, and then decide if the DIY or hiring route is right for you.

CHAPTER 6:

THE POWER OF SOCIAL MEDIA

"Social media is like a giant cocktail party. We're going to learn how to join the right conversations and make sure everyone notices you."

Choosing the Right Platforms for Your Audience

Social Media: It's a Big Party, But Where's Your Crowd?

Trying to be everywhere on social media is like showing up at a teenager's TikTok dance party dressed in a business suit and talking about your mortgage rates. Awkward! The key is finding the platforms where your ideal customers actually hang out.

Busting the "I Need to Be Everywhere" Myth

It's tempting to sign up for every social network under the sun. But spreading yourself thin = mediocre content and burnout. It's far better to do a few platforms WELL than to be on all of them poorly.

Step 1: Know Thy Audience

Go back to that super-detailed customer persona you created! Here's how demographics influence platform choice:

- Age:
  - » Gen Z and younger Millennials flock to TikTok and Instagram.
  - » Facebook skews older but still has a HUGE user base across generations.
  - » Location:

> » Some platforms are more popular in certain countries. Pinterest, for example, sees significant engagement in the US but less adoption elsewhere.

- Interests:

  > » LinkedIn is business networking central.

  > » Pinterest is a visual rabbit hole for recipes, DIY, and aesthetic inspiration.

- Type of Content:

  > » Instagram and TikTok are video-heavy.

  > » Long, written posts perform better on Facebook or a dedicated blog.

Step 2: Snoop on the Competition

Not to copy them blindly but to get a feel for what works within your industry. Ask yourself:

- Which platforms are they most active on? This gives you clues about where their audience likely is.

- What type of content gets the most engagement (comments, shares)?

- What's their overall vibe on each platform? Humorous, professional, behind-the-scenes?

Platform Deep Dives (With a Dash of Humor)

Let's break down some of the major players and the stereotypes associated with them:

- **Facebook:** The behemoth. Everyone from your grandma to your local businesses use it.

  - » **Audience:** Broad but skews older than some other platforms.

  - » **Best For:** Building a local following, customer service, long-form content, and running ads targeting super-specific demographics.

- **Instagram:** All about the aesthetic. Gorgeous photos and short videos rule.

  - » **Audience:** Younger crowd, loves visually appealing products and experiences.

  - » **Best For:** Businesses that have something pretty to show off – fashion, food, travel, interior design, etc.

- **X (Formerly Twitter):** Where news and witty commentary collide (and trolls sometimes lurk).

  - » **Audience:** Politically engaged, pop culture savvy, and those liking quick news bites.

  - » **Best For:** Real-time updates, engaging in trending conversations, brands with a sassy voice.

- **TikTok:** Short, often funny videos set to music. The algorithm is magical at showing the right content to the right people, even if you have zero followers.

- » **Audience:** HEAVILY Gen Z, but adoption by older users is growing.

- » **Best For:** Trends, challenges, showcasing products in a fun way, brands with a playful side.

- **LinkedIn:** Your digital resume and networking hub.

- » **Audience:** Professionals, B2B (business-to-business).

- » **Best For:** Building authority in your industry, sharing business-related content, job hunting, or posting openings.

Case Study: The Accidental TikTok Star

A small-town plumber started posting funny videos of himself on the job, explaining common problems in a relatable way. He BLEW UP on TikTok, gaining tons of local followers who became paying customers. Would he have found the same audience on LinkedIn? Probably not!

Don't Be Afraid to Experiment

Social media trends change fast. Dip your toe in a new platform, but with these caveats:

- **Set Goals:** What do you want to achieve? More brand awareness? Driving traffic to a website?

- **Give It Time:** Building a following takes consistency, not a few random posts.

- **Measure Results:** Are you getting engagement relevant to your business? Or just random likes that don't turn into customers?

Remember Your Brand Voice

While your tone might shift slightly between platforms, the core of your brand personality should shine through on all of them. The goal is to make your business recognizable no matter which social network someone encounters you on.

Content Strategies for Engagement

Stop Posting Boring Stuff! Content That Gets People Talking

Think social media is just a digital billboard for your latest sale? Snooze-fest! To truly stand out, you need content that makes people stop scrolling, laugh, think, and want to share with their friends. Let's get those engagement numbers soaring!

Engagement is Key: Why Bother?

- **The Algorithms Love It:** Most platforms reward posts with lots of likes, comments, and shares by showing them to more people... for free!

- **Builds Community:** Engaged followers become loyal customers and even advocates for your brand.

- **Insights Galore:** Comments tell you what your audience cares about, their pain points, and even what language they use.

Content Pillars: Your Engagement Foundation

Instead of random posting, have 3-5 broad categories your content fits into. This keeps you focused and helps your audience know what to expect. Examples:

- **Pillar 1: Educate:** Useful tips, how-tos related to your industry.

- **Pillar 2: Entertain:** Funny memes (make sure they're relevant to your niche!), relatable fails.

- **Pillar 3: Inspire:** Customer testimonials, quotes, before/after transformations.

- **Pillar 4: Behind-the-Scenes:** Show the human side of your business, introduce your team.

- **Pillar 5: Promote:** YES, some posts can be sales-y, but don't overdo this one!

Case Study: The Boring Accounting Firm Gets a Makeover

- **Old Content:** Dry blog posts about tax deadlines. *Yawn.*

- **Engagement Strategy:**

  » Pillar 1: Infographics simplifying complex tax law.

- » Pillar 2: Accountant memes for stressed-out business owners.

- » Pillar 3: Client spotlights celebrating successes.

- **The Result:** Their social media comes alive, people actually TAG their friends on posts, and inquiries for services increase.

Formats to Spice Things Up

- **Video, Video, Video:** Whether it's polished and edited or a quick "talking head" style, video outperforms plain text on most platforms.

- **Carousels:** Instagram's multiple-image format lets you tell mini-stories or provide more detail.

- **"Snackable" Content:** Short, attention-grabbing posts perfect for a quick scroll session.

- **User-Generated Content:** Ask customers to share pictures using your product – makes people feel seen and builds social proof.

Engagement Boosting Tactics

Beyond great content, try these techniques:

- **Ask Questions:** "What's your biggest struggle with X?" gets more conversation going than a statement.

- **Contests and Giveaways:** A well-structured one can bring new eyes to your page (think simple to enter and prize relevant to your ideal customer).

- **Respond to Comments:** Ignoring them is like snubbing someone at a party. Be responsive and genuine!

- **Use Hashtags Wisely:** Don't overdo it, and research which ones are used by your target audience.

- **Polls and Stories Features:** Great for quick feedback and building buzz around new things.

Beware of the Engagement Bait Trap

Posts like "Tag a friend who needs this!" might get artificial likes but rarely lead to meaningful engagement for your business. Focus on providing value first.

Content Calendars: Your Sanity Saver

Batching your content creation and using a scheduling tool (many have free options) lets you be consistent without social media taking over your life.

Inspiration When You're Stuck

- **Your FAQs:** Every question a customer has asked is potential content.

- **Google "Autocomplete":** Start typing a relevant search and see what suggestions pop up – those are things people actively wonder about!

- **Trend Watch:** What's going viral? Can you put a spin on it that connects to your business (without being cringey)?

Analyzing Your Results

Every platform has some level of analytics built in. Don't just post and forget! See:

- **Which posts BOMBED:** Learn from the flops to do better next time.

- **Your Engagement Stars:** What made those so successful? Replicate that magic!

- **Timing Matters:** Day of the week and even time of day can impact how many people see your content.

Social media is an ever-evolving beast. But the core principle stays the same: provide content that makes your ideal customer's social media feed a better place. Do that, and both the engagement and the sales will follow.

CHAPTER 7:

CONTENT MARKETING THAT WORKS

"Stop shouting 'Buy my stuff!' and start offering value. We'll explore content that attracts customers like magnets."

Blog Posts, Videos, Infographics, etc.

Content Marketing: Your Ticket to Becoming an Expert

Picture this: you need a new pair of hiking boots. Do you buy from the first store you stumble upon, or do some research – read reviews, watch trail test videos, and compare features? Content marketing is the equivalent of those helpful reviews and videos for your business.

Why Content Marketing Isn't Just "Blogging"

- **Builds Trust:** Consistently offering value for free positions you as the go-to source of information, even before someone's ready to buy.

- **Great for SEO:** Optimized blog posts help you rank in search results (see your SEO chapter!).

- **Versatile:** Content gets repurposed! A blog post could become an infographic, social media post, or even an email series.

The Content Powerhouse: Blog Posts

The workhorse of your content strategy. But please, don't make them textbook dull!

- **Solve Problems, Not Just Features:** "5 Ways to Style This Sweater" is more useful than listing its specs.

- **Storytelling Works:** Case studies, even in 'unsexy' industries, make it relatable.

- **Keywords + Readability:** SEO matters, but so does writing like a human, not a robot.

- **Visuals are Key:** Breaking up text with images, embedding videos... makes it more likely people actually finish reading.

Case Study: The Pet Store Blog That Became a Local Sensation

Instead of just pushing products, their blog posts focused on pet care tips, local dog-friendly spots, and interviews with adorable adoptable animals. This made them THE trusted resource, and people naturally shopped there when they needed pet supplies.

Video: The Star on the Rise

If blogging is the workhorse, video is the attention-grabbing show pony! Types to consider:

- **How-tos and Demos:** Perfect for showing your product in action or teaching a skill.

- **Short and Sweet is IN:** TikTok and Instagram Reels demand you keep it snappy. Long-form still works for YouTube.

- **Don't Be Afraid of Imperfect:** Behind-the-scenes peeks with your phone camera can be more engaging than a highly polished studio setup.

- **Captions and Subtitles:** Many people watch with sound off!

Infographics: Data Doesn't Have to Be Ugly

Great for:

- **Complex Topics:** Break down stats or processes in a visual, digestible way.

- **Shareability:** People love to share eye-catching infographics packed with useful info on social media.

- **Boosting Your Authority:** Makes your blog posts feel more weighty and well-researched.

Other Content Gems to Explore

- **Podcasts:** Great for niche audiences and building super-fans. Can be just audio or filmed as well.

- **Webinars:** Showcase your expertise LIVE, and collect emails of engaged participants for future marketing.

- **Customer Spotlights:** Written features, interviews, or even short videos humanize your brand and build social proof.

- **E-books/Guides:** Offer an in-depth download in exchange for an email address (grows your list!).

Content That Flops: Rookie Mistakes

- **All About YOU:** Nobody cares about your awards as much as how you solve THEIR problems.

- **Inconsistent:** One random blog post a year won't move the needle. Find a sustainable cadence.

- **Not Promoting It:** Creating amazing content is half the battle. Get it in front of people on social media, email, etc.

The "I'm Not Creative" Excuse

Let's bust this myth! You don't need to be the next Spielberg to do content marketing well.

- **Curation is Key:** Share relevant articles by others, adding your own take. This still positions you as knowledgeable.

- **Outsource What You Hate:** If writing makes you break out in hives, hire a pro. You focus on the ideas, they put it into words.

- **Tools Help!:** Canva makes infographic creation drag-and-drop easy. Stock footage websites add polish to your videos without needing fancy gear.

Content marketing is a marathon, not a sprint. Each piece of content is like planting a seed – some might sprout quickly, others may take time, but that garden will keep feeding your business for the long haul!

Distribution and Promotion

You Made Amazing Content... Now What? Getting Your Work Seen

Imagine spending hours crafting the perfect gourmet meal, and then leaving it to sit on the kitchen counter uneaten. That's what happens when you create amazing content but neglect distribution!

Distribution vs. Promotion: What's the Difference?

- **Distribution:** The channels where you put your content. This could be your own platforms (blog, social media) or others (guest posting, getting featured in articles).

- **Promotion:** Actively spreading the word about your content to reach a wider audience. This can be free or paid tactics.

Own Your Distribution Hub: Your Website

This is your home base, where you have full control. Make sure it's:

- **Optimized for SEO:** So the right people find your content through search.

- **Easy to Navigate:** Visitors should be able to find older blog posts and easily subscribe to your email list.

- **Share Buttons:** Make it one-click simple for people to share your content on their own social channels.

Extend Your Reach: Other Distribution Channels

- **Email Marketing:** Don't just blast sales! Share content highlights in your newsletter.

- **Guest Posting:** Write for other websites in your niche, tapping into their existing audience.

- **Social Media:** Yes, create original posts for each platform, BUT...

- **Repurpose the Heck Out of Things:** A blog post becomes post threads, an infographic, even a short video script.

- **Online Communities:** Be a genuine, helpful participant in relevant Facebook groups or forums. Subtly promote your content where appropriate.

Case Study: The Infographic that Went Viral

A small wellness brand created an infographic on "7 Signs You're Overly Stressed." They:

- Shared it on their own social media channels with relevant hashtags.

- Promoted it in their email newsletter.

- Reached out to bloggers and online magazines in the wellness space, and several shared it with their much larger audience.

Result: A huge traffic spike to their website and tons of new email subscribers!

Free Promotion Power-Ups

- **Leverage Your Network:** Ask friends, colleagues, and happy customers to share. A personal recommendation goes far.

- **Use Your Email Signature:** Link to your latest blog post or awesome piece of content. Changes with every email you send!

- **Create Quote Graphics:** Visually appealing snippets of your content are highly shareable on social.

- **HARO (Help a Reporter Out):** Journalists often seek experts to quote. Could lead to media features!

Paid Promotion: Worth It?

It depends. Here's when it makes sense:

- **You Know Your Audience Targeting:** Ads work best when super-specific to who you want to reach.

- **You Have a Proven Funnel:** Don't pay to send people to a janky website that doesn't convert viewers to clients.

- **You Can Measure Results:** If ads cost > money earned, something's gotta change.

Start with Low-Budget Experiments

- **"Boosting" Social Media Posts:** Easy way to dip your toe in. Target a niche audience likely to be interested.

- **PPC Ads (Pay-Per-Click):** Your text ads show up on search results for specific keywords. Good for intent-based searches ("best hiking boots near me").

The Content Treadmill: Creation AND Promotion

Content marketing is an ongoing effort. You'll get better over time at understanding what resonates with your audience and finding distribution channels that deliver the best results.

Here's a simple workflow to avoid feeling overwhelmed:

- **Batch Your Content Creation:** Set aside focused time to write several blog posts, or film multiple videos at once.

- **Repurpose and Pre-Schedule:** While the content is fresh in your brain, turn it into social media graphics, email snippets, etc.

- **Automate Where Possible:** Tools like Hootsuite let you schedule social shares in advance.

- **Actively Engage:** Spend some time each day responding to comments, participating in discussions... this builds relationships AND exposes you to even more potential followers/customers.

PART III:

BEYOND THE BASICS

CHAPTER 8:

EMAIL MARKETING DONE RIGHT

"Email is far from dead! Let's use it to build relationships, not annoy people. Get ready to make your inbox a revenue generator."

Building a List, Segmentation, and Effective Messaging

Email: The Marketing Darling That Refuses to Die

Every few years, some trendy new platform promises to make email obsolete. And yet, email remains a marketing powerhouse! Why?

- **You Own the Relationship:** Social algorithms change, accounts get hacked... but your email list is yours.

- **Direct Line to Customers:** People check their inboxes. Your message cuts through the social media noise.

- **Fantastic ROI:** It's surprisingly affordable compared to some other marketing channels.

But here's the thing: blasting generic messages to everyone on your list is the digital equivalent of shouting into a void. Let's get strategic!

Step 1: Grow Your Tribe

People must OPT IN to receive your emails (legally, and it builds trust!). How to entice them:

- **The Lead Magnet:** An irresistible freebie in exchange for their email. Could be an e-book, checklist, exclusive discount, etc.

- **Content Upgrades:** Blog post on "5 Design Mistakes"? Offer a bonus cheat sheet download within the post itself.

- **Simple Pop-Up Forms:** Yes, they can be annoying if done poorly, but tasteful ones with a clear benefit convert well.

- **Make Subscribing Easy:** Include a signup form on your website's sidebar, footer, and a prominent "Subscribe" page.

Step 2: Segmentation = Superpowers

Dividing your list into smaller groups based on interests, behavior, etc., lets you send the RIGHT message to the right people. Here's how:

- **Signup Surveys:** Ask about their pain points or which topics they're most interested in.

- **Track Behavior:** Did they click on links about a certain product? Add them to a segment focused on that category.

- **Location and Demographics:** If you're a local biz, sending everyone an event invite is useless to those far away.

Example: The Plant Shop's Email Magic

- **Segment 1:** New subscribers
  - » Welcome email series introducing the brand, sharing a coupon.

- **Segment 2:** Purchased specific plant types
  - » Emails with care tips tailored to those plants, plus suggestions of related accessories.

- **Segment 3:** Abandoned their cart
  - » Reminder email, maybe even a small extra discount to nudge them to complete the purchase.

Step 3: Don't Be a Spammy Salesperson

The fastest way to that "Unsubscribe" button? Always bombarding people with pitches.

- **The 80/20 Rule:** 80% valuable content, 20% promotion is a good balance.

- **Subject Lines Matter!:** Boring ones get ignored. Pique curiosity without being clickbait-y.

- **Personality Please:** Write like you talk to a friend, not a corporate robot.

- **Make it Scannable:** Big blocks of text are intimidating. Bullet points, headings, and images help.

- **The Power of Storytelling:** Even when selling, weave in anecdotes and case studies to make it relatable.

Case Study: The Freelance Writer Who Niched Down

She started by emailing everyone on her list with any potential writing gig. Open rates were dismal. Then she:

- Segmented clients by industry (tech, health, etc.)

- Tailored her subject lines AND the jobs she promoted within each email to those specialties.

Result: Engagement skyrocketed! Clients felt she truly understood their needs, making them more likely to hire her.

Quick Tech Tips

- **Choose a Provider:** Mailchimp has a decent free plan, others offer more features as you grow.

- **Focus on Deliverability:** Avoid spammy language and make sure people can unsubscribe easily – it protects your sender reputation.

- **Test and Measure!:** Which subject lines get opened the most? Experiment to improve over time.

The Ethical Side of Email

- **Respect Permission:** Never buy lists or automatically add people without their consent.

- **Don't Be a Ghost:** Email consistently enough that people remember who you are, but not so often that you get annoying.

- **The "Unsubscribe" Option:** Make it easy to find, and honor those requests promptly.

Email marketing may not be the newest kid on the block, but when done strategically, it's still the best way to nurture potential customers, build loyalty, and drive sales for the long haul.

.

CHAPTER 9:

THE ART OF STORYTELLING

"Facts tell, stories sell. Let's turn your business into a captivating tale that customers can't resist."

Using Narratives to Connect with Your Audience

Why Facts Tell, But Stories Sell

Think of your marketing as a friendly conversation, not a stiff lecture. Stories are what make people lean in, relate, and actually remember what you're saying long after the sales pitch is forgotten.

Our Brains Are Wired for Stories

Cavemen didn't share spreadsheets around the campfire – they shared tales of epic hunts and narrow escapes. Why?

- **Emotional Connection:** Stories tap into feelings, not just logic. We root for the underdog, laugh along with relatable mishaps, and feel the satisfaction of a problem solved.

- **Creates Vivid Imagery:** "Our software streamlines workflow" is meh. Describing a harried team drowning in paperwork before vs. their newfound zen after IS a story.

- **Boosts Memory:** We recall stories far better than random facts or bullet points.

Don't Confuse "Story" With Cheesy Fairy Tale

No need to make up epic sagas about the founding of your company. Authenticity is key! Types of stories to leverage:

- **The Origin Story:** How did you get into this business? Was it a lifelong dream or an "aha" moment that changed everything?

- **Customer Successes:** Instead of dry case studies, paint a picture of someone's life BEFORE and AFTER your product/service.

- **Overcoming Obstacles:** Share a blunder you learned from, or a time things seemed bleak, but you kept going. Vulnerability makes you relatable.

- **Behind-the-Scenes:** People love peeking behind the curtain! Showing your process builds trust and makes your work feel less abstract.

Case Study: The Boring Tech Company Gets a Soul

Their old marketing materials were full of jargon most people didn't understand. Then they started sharing:

- **Employee Profiles:** Highlighting the diverse personalities and talents on their team.

- **"Day in the Life" Videos:** Showing how their software is actually used in a relatable (and kinda funny) way.

- **Client Transformations:** "Before our tech, their team was miserable. Now they get home in time for dinner!"

Result: People began seeing them as humans who solve problems, not some faceless corporation.

Storytelling Doesn't Have to Be Words Only

- **Video:** Customer testimonials or short documentaries about your process are powerful.

- **Infographics:** A timeline of your company's growth or a step-by-step visual of how something works can be a story in itself!

- **Social Media:** A series of images with captions can draw people in, especially on Instagram.

Storytelling in Action: How to Apply This

Let's make it practical! Here's how to add a story element across your marketing:

- **Your Website's "About" Page:** Don't be a corporate drone. Share your WHY, not just what you do.

- **Email Newsletters:** Instead of just sales, a short customer success story becomes content people look forward to.

- **Product Descriptions:** "Soft fabric" is blah. "Perfect for curling up with a good book on a rainy day" paints the picture!

- **Social Media Captions:** Go beyond pretty pics. Share the mini-drama of creating the product or a funny customer question.

- **Ads:** A customer quote about how your service changed their life is more impactful than shouting about your features.

Warnings Before You Embark

- **Don't Force It:** If a genuine story doesn't leap out, that's okay. Focus on clear, benefit-driven messaging instead.

- **Embellishment = Bad Idea:** Stay truthful. People sniff out B.S., and it damages your reputation.

- **Respect Privacy:** Always get permission before sharing customer stories, even if you anonymize them.

Start Small, the "Storyteller Muscle" Grows

Look for opportunities to weave tiny bits of narrative into what you're already doing. Soon, it'll become second nature. You might be surprised at how a simple shift from features-yelling to relatable storytelling transforms your marketing results AND makes the whole process way more fun!

CHAPTER 10:

MEASURING YOUR RESULTS

"Marketing isn't guesswork. We'll dive into the numbers that show you what works and what's wasting your time."

Key Metrics to Track

Metrics: Decoding the Marketing Dashboard

Imagine driving a car blindfolded. Kinda terrifying, right? That's marketing without tracking metrics. Data might not be the sexiest topic, but it tells you whether you're cruising toward your dream destination or about to careen off a cliff.

Let's demystify those dashboards full of numbers and make sure you're focused on what truly matters for your business.

Not ALL Metrics Are Equal

It's tempting to obsess over vanity metrics – things like follower counts or page likes. Those feel good, but don't always equal dollars in your bank account. We need to dig deeper!

Key Metrics Categories

Let's break them down in order of a customer's typical journey:

- **Reach/Awareness Metrics**

  » **Website Traffic:** How many people visit, which pages get the most attention, where are visitors coming from (search, social, etc.).

  » **Social Media Impressions:** How many times your content was displayed (even if no clicks).

  » **Follower Growth:** Useful over time, but not the end-all-be-all metric.

- **Engagement Metrics**

  - » **Likes, Comments, Shares:** Do people actually interact, or just passively scroll past?

  - » **Click-Through Rate (CTR):** On ads, emails, etc. A high CTR means your message resonated.

  - » **Time on Site/Video Watch Time:** Are people quickly bouncing away, or truly engaged?

- **Conversion Metrics**

  - » **THE Most Important Category!** This is where the rubber hits the road.

  - » **Sales:** Duh! The ultimate goal.

  - » **Lead Form Submissions:** If you collect email addresses before a sale, track this.

  - » **Webinar Registrations/Downloads:** Shows strong interest in your content.

  - » **Shopping Cart Abandonment Rate:** Identifies fixable leaks in your sales process.

Case Study: The Influencer Trap

A small biz owner hired an influencer with tons of followers to promote them. Tons of likes and comments on the post... but sales barely budged. Why?

- The influencer's audience wasn't a good match for the product (wrong demographics, interests).

- The campaign focused on reach, not conversions (no strong call to action).

Lesson: Huge follower count is meaningless if it's not YOUR target customer. Smaller, niche audiences can be more profitable!

Metrics that Matter: By Business Type

Not every business needs to track the exact same things:

- **E-commerce:** Sales, average order value, shopping cart abandonment rate are crucial.

- **Service-Based:** Leads generated, where they came from, close rate (how many leads turn into paying clients).

- **Content Creator/Blogger:** Website traffic sources, affiliate link clicks, email open rates tell you what's working.

Analytics Tools: Your Data Sidekicks

- **Google Analytics (Free!):** Tracks a ton of website data. Takes time to master, but it's incredibly powerful.

- **Social Media Insights:** Built into most platforms, giving you basic engagement and demographic breakdowns.

- **Email Marketing Provider Reports:** Open rates, click-throughs, and unsubscribes galore.

- **Paid Ads Power:** Facebook Ads Manager, etc., provide granular data on campaign performance.

The "So What?!" Factor

Don't just stare at numbers, ASK:

- What's working REALLY well? Let's do more of that!

- What's flopping? Time to change tactics or ditch it altogether.

- Trends over time? Is your Instagram engagement steadily increasing as you improve your content?

- Are the RIGHT people finding you? Lots of website traffic is useless if they're not your ideal customer.

Beware of Analysis Paralysis

It's easy to get stuck tweaking tiny things. Here's how to avoid that:

- **Focus on 3-5 Key Metrics:** These will shift depending on your current marketing goals.

- **Set a Review Schedule:** Weekly or monthly deep dives are better than obsessing daily.

- **Actionable Insights Only:** If a number doesn't help you make a decision to change something, stop tracking it for a while.

Marketing metrics are your road map. Embrace the data, use it to make informed decisions, and you'll find yourself reaching your business goals faster (and with a lot less random flailing in the dark!).

Introduction to Analytics Tools

Unlocking the Secrets of Your Marketing: Analytics Tools

Think of analytics tools as your very own superhero squad. They reveal things you can't see with the naked eye – like whether your website turns people into raving fans or makes them run away screaming. This knowledge is your superpower!

Why Analytics Matter (Beyond Being Nosy)

- **Stop Guessing, Start Knowing:** Was last month's sales spike thanks to that brilliant email or a lucky fluke? Data tells the story.

- **Test and Improve:** Should you spend more on Facebook ads or focus on creating killer blog posts? Analytics help you make informed choices.

- **Maximize Your Budget:** If you know $1 spent on a certain tactic brings back $5, wouldn't you want to invest more there?

- **Spot Problems Early:** Website traffic suddenly tanking? Time to investigate BEFORE you lose a ton of potential customers.

Popular Analytics Tools & Their Superpowers

Let's meet the main heroes of your data detective team:

- **Google Analytics 4 (GA4): The Big Kahuna**

» **Focus:** All things website! Traffic, visitor behavior, where they're coming from, and way more.

» **Complexity:** Can be overwhelming for beginners, but there are TONS of free tutorials online.

» **Cost:** Free version is surprisingly powerful, paid version unlocks even more advanced features.

» **Best For:** Pretty much anyone with a website needs GA4 to track the basics.

- **Social Media Insights: Built-In Intel**

  » **Focus:** Performance of your Facebook, Instagram, X, etc. pages and individual posts.

  » **Complexity:** Pretty user-friendly for seeing basic engagement metrics at a glance.

  » **Cost:** Included with the platforms themselves.

  » **Best For:** Quick check-ins on what's getting likes/ comments and basic audience demographics.

- **Email Marketing Tools: Your List's Lifeblood**

  » **Focus:** How people interact with your email campaigns (opens, clicks, unsubscribes...)

  » **Complexity:** Varies between providers, but most have easy-to-understand reports.

  » **Cost:** Built into the price of your email marketing service (Mailchimp, ConvertKit, etc.)

- » **Best For:** Seeing which subject lines rock, optimizing send times, and identifying your super-fans.

- **Paid Advertising Platforms: Tracking Your Spend**
    - » **Focus:** Deep data on how ads on Facebook, Google, etc. are performing.
    - » **Complexity:** Can get complex, especially when you're running multiple campaigns.
    - » **Cost:** Included with the ad platforms themselves.
    - » **Best For:** Determining if your ad dollars are actually resulting in leads and sales.

Case Study: The Accidental Data Geek

A small boutique owner thought she was "bad at numbers." But when she started exploring her Shopify store's built-in analytics, she discovered:

- Her top-selling items had tiny profit margins, while a few niche products were ignored but way more lucrative!

- Most sales happened on weekends, so that became her promo focus, not random midweek blasts.

- Identifying her best customer demographics helped her target Facebook ads with laser precision.

Result: Increased profits without MORE work, just smarter work informed by data.

Taming the Data Beast: Tips for Beginners

» **Start Simple:** Pick 1-2 tools to master first. Trying to do everything at once is a recipe for overwhelm.

» **Focus on Key Metrics:** What are the 3-5 numbers most important to your current business goals? Track those religiously.

» **It's a Journey, Not a Destination:** Your data needs will change as you grow. Regularly re-evaluate what to track.

» **Don't Be Afraid to Ask:** Tons of free tutorials, blog posts, and communities exist to help you understand analytics.

A Word on Privacy

With great data power comes great responsibility!

- **Respect Regulations:** Things like GDPR in Europe govern how you collect and use customer data.

- **Transparency is Key:** Have a clear privacy policy on your website, and make it easy for people to opt out of tracking if they desire.

Analytics tools can feel intimidating at first, but the potential benefits to your business are HUGE. Start by dipping your toe in, track a few key things, and let the insights guide your marketing decisions. You might be surprised at how quickly you transform from data-phobe to data-driven marketing whiz!

CHAPTER 11:

PAID ADVERTISING (OPTIONAL)

"Ready to give your marketing a boost? We'll demystify paid advertising and discuss if it's the right move for you."

Brief Overview of Options

Paid Advertising: The Marketing Fast Lane (But Proceed with Caution)

Organic marketing (through content, SEO, etc.) is like planting a garden. It yields delicious results but takes time. Paid ads are like buying a pre-made salad – quick but can get soggy if you choose the wrong one! Let's do a quick breakdown of the major players.

Google Ads: When Search Intent Is High

- **How They Work:** Your text ads show up at the top of search results for specific keywords people type in.

- **Best For:** When someone is actively searching for a solution to their problem ("best hiking boots for wide feet," "plumber near me").

- **Cost:** Pay-per-click (PPC). You can set daily budgets, but costs vary wildly between competitive search terms.

- **Watch Out For:** Clicks don't equal customers. If your website or offer is bad, you'll burn through cash.

Case Study: The Invisible Locksmith

A locksmith was getting no leads from his website despite ranking decently on Google. Turns out, no one was searching for his outdated keywords like "house keys cut."

He launched a small Google Ads campaign for "emergency lockout service Lombard" and his phone started ringing off the hook!

Social Media Ads: Laser-Focused Targeting

- **How They Work:** Those ads slipping into your Instagram feed! Various formats (image, video, carousel, etc.).

- **Best For:** Targeting based on interests, demographics, behaviors... even if someone isn't actively searching at that moment.

- **Cost:** Can be budget-friendly, but the major platforms get pricier as more businesses compete.

- **Watch Out For:** It's easy to target the WRONG audience, wasting ad spend on people unlikely to convert.

Types of Social Media Ads

- **Boosting Posts:** Simplest option, but often the least effective. Better to create ads specifically designed to stand out from organic content.

- **Lead Generation Ads:** Collect email addresses within the platform itself, good for growing your list.

- **Retargeting Ads:** Show ads ONLY to people who've already visited your website or interacted with you in the past (those "stalker ads" that follow you around!).

Case Study: The Local Biz Winning vs. Big Chains

A small yoga studio couldn't compete on Google Ads with national brands. However, Facebook ads targeting women within a 5-mile radius, interested in fitness, who also liked Whole Foods (implying they had the income for wellness services) worked like magic!

Is Paid Advertising Right for You?

Ask yourself these tough questions first:

- **Do I have a KILLER offer?** No amount of ads will save a crappy product or confusing sales page.

- **Is my website ready for traffic?** Do people immediately "get" what I offer and know how to buy/contact me?

- **Can I handle the leads?** Inquiry floods are useless if you have no system for follow-up.

- **Am I willing to experiment?** Rarely do you hit a home run with your first ad. It takes testing and tweaking.

When Paid Ads Make Sense

- **Scaling a Proven System:** You already get sales organically, ads amplify that.

- **Speed is Necessary:** Launching a time-sensitive promotion or new product.

- **Hyperlocal Targeting:** Ideal for businesses with a tight geographic focus.

- **You Have the Budget AND Skills:** Hiring an expert can be worth it if you don't have the time to DIY.

Start Small, Test, Iterate

Paid advertising can be a powerful tool, but it's NOT a substitute for good organic marketing. Here's how to dip your toe in:

- **Pick ONE Platform:** Don't try to master them all at once.

- **Tightly Focused Campaign:** Target a super-specific audience and have a single goal (promoting a webinar, etc.).

- **Track EVERYTHING:** Did those clicks turn into leads? Did those leads turn into sales?

Paid advertising is a complex beast. But by starting small, focusing on the right audience, and relentlessly tracking your results, it can be a way to accelerate your business growth and leave your competitors wondering what your secret sauce is!

CHAPTER 12:

BUILDING A MARKETING MINDSET

"The best marketers never stop learning. We'll cover how to stay 'in the know' so your business is always ahead of the curve."

Staying Up-to-Date with Trends

The Marketing Hamster Wheel: Why Keeping Up Matters

Remember when everyone on Facebook suddenly had those weird Bitmoji avatars? Or that week Clubhouse was the hot new thing? Marketing trends move FAST. Ignoring them makes your business look like that person still rocking frosted tips... well-intentioned, but out of touch.

But... Isn't "Good Marketing" Timeless?

Yes and no. Core principles (understanding your customer, etc.) always ring true. BUT how those play out changes. Think of marketing trends like fashion:

- **Basics are Always in:** A flattering, well-made dress works across decades. That's like focusing on customer needs.

- **Trendy Pieces Elevate:** Neon leg warmers? Only in the '80s. That's like a viral TikTok challenge, fun but fleeting.

- **Ignoring Trends Ages You:** Rocking shoulder pads in 2023 is a choice... a questionable one. Same with ignoring the rise of video marketing.

Why You Should Care (Even a Little Bit)

- **Meet Customers Where They Are:** If teens flock to a new app, but you're not there, you miss out on a whole market.

- **Efficiency Boost:** New tools or platforms can streamline your efforts and get better results for less work.

- **Competitive Edge:** While rivals fumble with the latest trend, you swoop in looking like the savvy pro.

- **Avoid Embarrassing Flops:** Remember when every brand awkwardly shoehorned "Gangnam Style" into tweets? Oof.

Case Study: The "Too Cool for School" Cafe

Quirky cafe owner prided himself on being anti-social media. "Good coffee speaks for itself," he declared. Meanwhile, a competitor down the street started:

- Posting drool-worthy latte art on Instagram, tagging their location.

- Running contests for the best customer-submitted photo of their cozy atmosphere.

- Partnering with local influencers, offering a "secret menu" item only revealed to the influencers' followers.

Result: Long lines at the trendy spot, while the old-school cafe's customer base aged along with its owner.

Trend-Spotting Without Losing Your Mind

The internet is a firehose of "The Next Big Thing!" predictions. Here's how to stay informed, not overwhelmed:

- **Follow Smart People:** Find industry blogs, newsletters, or podcasts known for thoughtful analysis, not just hype.

- **Competitor Observation:** What are businesses like yours trying? Reverse-engineer their successes (and avoid their mistakes).

- **Customer Feedback is Gold:** Ask them what social platforms they use, what kind of content they enjoy, etc.

- **Niche Down:** Trying to be an expert on ALL marketing trends is a recipe for burnout. Focus on what's most relevant to YOUR target audience.

Ways to Tap into Trends

- **Repurpose with a Twist:** Jump on a viral TikTok audio trend but use it to showcase your product in a unique way.

- **Don't Force It:** If short-form video makes you want to hurl, there are other ways to stay current.

- **Experiment, Then Evaluate:** Tried a hot new tactic and it flopped? That's data too! Now you know where to focus your energy.

"Trendy" Doesn't Equal "Abandon Your Brand"

It's tempting to chase every shiny object. Here's how to filter what's worth pursuing:

- **Does it align with your values?** Hopping on a sleazy meme trend damages trust, even if it gets views.

- **Can you execute it WELL?** Half-hearted attempts are worse than doing nothing at all.

- **Will your IDEAL customer care?** Gen Z slang might alienate your target audience of retirees.

Trend-Spotting Resources (To Get You Started)

- **Industry-Specific Publications:** Adweek for a broad view, or niche down (like Beauty Independent for beauty businesses).

- **Platform News Blogs:** Facebook, Instagram, etc. often announce algorithm changes or new features.

- **Google Trends:** See what people are searching for, compare the popularity of terms over time. Fun AND useful!

The FUN Part of Marketing

Staying on top of trends keeps things fresh. It forces you out of your comfort zone, sparks creativity, and can attract a whole new wave of customers who see you as the cool brand that "gets it." Now, go forth and conquer those viral challenges (or at least understand why your teenage intern is so obsessed with them)!

Continuous Learning and Adaptation

Embrace the Marketing Pivot: Why Change is Your Friend

Imagine if doctors still used the "treatments" from the 1800s (blood-letting, anyone?). Cringe! The marketing world evolves just as fast. Being open to learning and adapting is what separates thriving businesses from those stuck in a dusty time capsule.

Why the "We've Always Done It This Way" Mentality is Dangerous

- **Customer Expectations Shift:** What dazzled folks five years ago feels basic now. Think about how quickly websites went from text-heavy to the image-focused designs we expect today.

- **Algorithms are Fickle Beasts:** The tactics that got results on social media last year might be penalized today.

- **Competitors Innovate While You Stagnate:** They're busy stealing your customers with those shiny new strategies you refuse to learn.

- **Getting Stuck in a Rut Kills Creativity:** Marketing should be FUN! Trying new things sparks fresh ideas and prevents burnout.

Case Study: The Newspaper vs. the Nimble Blogger

- **The Dinosaur:** Local newspaper relied on print ads, reluctant to embrace digital. Declining readership = fewer ad sales = a slow, painful death spiral.

- **The Adaptable Upstart:** A food blogger started with simple reviews, then built:

  » An email list offering exclusive recipes to subscribers.

  » Partnerships with local restaurants for sponsored content.

  » Online courses teaching food photography.

» Brand deals based on her engaged social media following.

Who do you think businesses flocked to for advertising? The one stuck in the past, or the innovator finding new ways to reach the audience?

Continuous Learning Doesn't Have to Be Torture

- **Small, Sustainable Wins:** Trying to overhaul EVERYTHING overnight leads to overwhelm. Fifteen minutes a day dedicated to learning is better than an annual cram session you dread.

- **Focus on Your "Why":** What results would get you EXCITED? (More website traffic, a fully-booked schedule...) This motivates you to learn the HOW.

- **Find Your Learning Style:** Hate webinars? Podcasts or short blog posts might be your jam. Experiment!

- **Leverage Free Resources:** Tons of blogs, YouTube tutorials, and even free mini-courses exist.

Adapting in Action: Examples

- **Customer Feedback Changes the Game:** Getting comments about confusing product descriptions? Time to update your website copy, stat!

- **A/B Testing:** Try two subject lines, see which gets opened more. Small tweak, potentially big impact.

- **Ditching the Flops:** Spent hours on elaborate blog posts no one reads? Pivot to short-form video your audience DOES engage with.

Skill Sets That Never Go Out of Style

While the specific platforms and tactics change, these foundational skills will always serve you well:

- **Copywriting:** The ability to write persuasively, whether it's an ad or an email subject line.

- **Basic Design Principles:** Even if you hire out, understanding good vs. bad design helps you make smart choices.

- **Data Analysis:** Don't be afraid of numbers! The ability to understand what's working and what's not is invaluable.

- **The Human Touch:** Tools automate, but genuine connection with your customers is what builds loyalty.

Resources to Kickstart Your Learning

- **Industry Leaders:** Who do YOU look to for advice in your niche? Follow their blogs, courses, etc.

- **Your Own Data:** What content performed well in the past? Why? Replicate those wins.

- **"Beginner's Mind" Communities:** Facebook groups, subreddits, etc., where it's okay to ask "dumb" questions are incredibly supportive.

The Marketer's Mantra: Test, Tweak, Repeat

Even the "gurus" experiment. Things flop. That's part of the process! What sets successful marketers apart is:

- **They Don't Take Failure Personally:** A campaign bombs? Cool, now you know what NOT to do next time.

- **Curiosity Fuels Growth:** That "Huh, I wonder what would happen if..." mindset leads to breakthroughs.

- **Staying Humble:** There's ALWAYS more to learn. Even seasoned pros keep an open mind to new trends and strategies.

Marketing is a journey, not a destination. The moment you think you've got it all figured out is the moment you start to fall behind. Embrace change, stay curious, and the most intimidating marketing concepts will soon become your most powerful tools for growth!

CONCLUSION

You've Got the Power!

Okay, maybe you won't sprout magical marketing wings overnight, but you now have the foundation to transform from feeling overwhelmed to being in control of growing your business.

Think back to the beginning of this guide. Did terms like "SEO" or "content strategy" make you break out in a cold sweat? Now, you can not only define them but see how they fit into the big picture of attracting and keeping your dream customers.

The Journey, Not the Finish Line

There's no point where you'll officially "graduate" from needing to learn about marketing. It's as dynamic as your business itself! The good news is, with the tools and mindset you've developed, this ongoing evolution feels more like an exciting adventure than a chore.

Small Wins, Big Impact

Remember, you don't need to implement every single thing at once. Here's how to make this actionable without giving yourself an ulcer:

- **Pick ONE area to improve:** Is your website woefully outdated? Do you finally get what a customer persona is and need to create yours?

- **Set a realistic timeline:** Change takes time, so break down that big goal into bite-sized steps.

- **Celebrate the wins along the way:** First email newsletter sent? Ten new Instagram followers? Pat yourself on the back!

You Are NOT Alone

The marketing landscape is vast, but there's a vibrant community ready to help:

- **Free Resources Abound:** Blogs, tutorials, and forums exist for every niche imaginable. A simple Google search can solve most dilemmas.

- **Asking = Receiving:** Most business owners are happy to share what's worked for them (and what hasn't to save you the pain!),

- **Hire Help When It Makes Sense:** Not a DIY person? Delegating to a pro frees up your time to focus on what you do best – running your business.

The Secret Sauce: Authenticity

Yes, we've covered strategy and tactics. But the most important "marketing skill" to cultivate is simply being yourself. Customers are drawn to genuine passion and personality. Let that shine through alongside your newfound marketing knowledge, and you've got a recipe for unstoppable success!

Recap of Key Concepts

From Marketing Muggle to Master: Your Journey Revisited

Whoa, you've come a long way! Remember feeling lost in a sea of buzzwords and vaguely discouraged by those slickly produced ads you could never hope to replicate? Let's recap the major milestones and remind you just how powerful your newfound marketing knowledge truly is.

Chapter 1 & 2: The "Why" Before the "How"

- **Know Thy Customer (And Thyself!):** We dove into ideal customer personas and value propositions. No more shouting about your features into a void but speaking directly to the hearts of those who truly need what you offer.

- **Branding Basics:** Your logo, colors, and voice aren't just about being pretty; they make you instantly recognizable and build trust way faster than generic marketing blah-blah-blah.

Chapters 3 & 4: The Art of the Funnel

- **It's a Journey, Not a Mugging:** Understanding the stages of awareness, interest, consideration, and decision was an eye-opener, right? This lets you deliver the right message at the right time.

- **Luring Them In:** From enticing social posts to search-optimized blog articles, you now have a toolbox of tactics to pull people into your orbit.

Chapters 5, 6, & 7: Channels and Content

- **Your Website:** The Home Base: We tackled why good design and user experience matter as much as your eloquently written "About" page.

- **Social Media Power (Used Wisely):** Choosing the right platforms for YOUR audience and content strategies to make them actually pay off (not just a time suck) is a game-changer.

- **Content is King:** But only if it's GOOD content. Blog posts, videos, infographics... all are tools to become the go-to expert in your field.

Chapters 8 & 9: Getting Personal

- **Email Isn't Dead, You're Doing It Wrong:** We busted the myth of spammy blasts and learned segmentation, delivering value, and the power of a catchy subject line. Your subscribers might actually look forward to your emails now!

- **The Magic of Storytelling:** Facts and figures are fine, but stories are what make people remember you, root for you, and ultimately, pull out their wallets in support.

Chapters 10, 11, & 12: Beyond the Basics

- **Data:** Your New Best Friend: Metrics might have seemed scary, but now you know which numbers truly matter, and how to use them to make informed decisions (no more throwing spaghetti at the wall and hoping something sticks!).

- **Paid Ads: Proceed with Caution:** We touched on Google Ads, social media ads, and when they make sense for your business... often AFTER you've got a solid organic marketing foundation.

- **Marketing Never Sleeps:** Trends change, so we covered ways to stay up-to-date and the importance of adaptability. This ensures you're always ahead of the curve, not scrambling to catch up.

Case Study: The Transformation

Let's imagine "Before" and "After" versions of a small business owner:

- **Before:** Random social media posts, a hastily made website, and hoping word-of-mouth would magically lead to sales. Feeling stressed and vaguely like a failure.

- **After:** Crystal-clear target audience, a redesigned website that speaks to their pain points, a consistent content schedule on the RIGHT platforms, and email sequences that nurture potential customers along their journey. Confidence is up, and so are profits!

It's Not Magic, It's LEARNED

The best marketers weren't born with this knowledge. They started where you are now – curious, a bit overwhelmed, but determined. The difference? They took action, one step at a time.

Where to Go From Here

- **Pick Your Next Focus Area:** Don't try to do it all at once! What's the ONE thing that would move the needle most for your business? Dive deeper into that.

- **Join a Community:** Entrepreneur groups, niche-specific forums... surrounding yourself with others on the journey makes it way more fun and keeps you accountable.

- **Implementation Beats Information:** You could read marketing books forever, but applying what you learn, even imperfectly, is how REAL growth happens.

This guide gave you the road map. Now, the most exciting part of the adventure begins – forging your own unique path to marketing success. You've got this!

Marketing is an Ongoing Process

The Hamster Wheel of Joy? Why Marketing Never Truly Ends

You've reached the end of this guide, feeling armed with knowledge! But here's the thing: while you can pat yourself on the back for leveling up your marketing game, the work isn't really "done." Don't despair; think of it like tending a beautiful garden, not a one-time chore.

Why the "Set It and Forget It" Dream is a Lie

Sadly, you won't reach a point where customers magically flock to you on autopilot while you sip margaritas on a beach (well, maybe someday, but it takes sustained work to get there!). Here's why marketing requires ongoing attention:

- **Competitors Get Savvy:** They're not sitting still either. Staying ahead means continuous innovation to maintain your edge.

- **Customer Needs Change:** What worked like gangbusters last year might fall flat now due to economic shifts, new trends, etc. Adaptability is key.

- **Algorithms are Fickle Beasts:** Remember how that Facebook strategy crushed it? And then suddenly... crickets? Each platform's rules evolve; you gotta roll with the digital punches.

- **New Opportunities Emerge:** Maybe a hot new social network becomes THE place to reach your ideal audience. Early adopters reap the biggest rewards.

Case Study: The Snoozer vs. the Innovator

- **Business #1:** Built a decent website in 2010, did some basic SEO, then... nothing. It converts poorly, ranks low in search results, and reflects an outdated brand image.

- **Business #2:** Actively updates their website, tweaks their offerings based on customer feedback, and experiments with content on trending platforms.

Who do you think will thrive long-term? The one stuck in the past or the one embracing evolution?

"Ongoing" Doesn't Mean "Overwhelm"

It's important to find a sustainable rhythm. Here's how to make it manageable:

- **Focus on the High-Leverage Activities:** What moves the needle most for YOUR business? Ruthlessly prioritize those.

- **Create Systems:** Batching content creation, using scheduling tools, and having templates saves time and brainpower in the long run.

- **Review Regularly:** Set aside time (monthly, quarterly) to analyze your data. Are you spending time on things with little return? Ditch or tweak them!

- **Outsource What You Hate:** If writing makes you break out in hives, but you're a video whiz, find ways to delegate the pain points.

Examples of Ongoing Marketing Efforts

Let's make this practical. Here's the kind of stuff you'll ALWAYS have on your marketing to-do list:

- **Content Creation:** Fresh blog posts, social updates, videos, etc., keep your audience engaged and attract new eyeballs.

- **Search Engine Optimization:** It's not a one-time fix; you need to monitor your rankings and adapt as Google changes the rules.

- **Nurturing Your List:** Regular newsletters with value (not just pitches) build the "know, like, and trust" factor.

- **Community Engagement:** Responding to comments, participating in forums... shows you're a real person who cares, not a faceless corporation.

- **Testing and Tweaking:** Always try A/B versions of ads, landing pages, etc. Even small improvements add up to a big win over time.

The Growth Mindset Shift

The most successful business owners stop seeing marketing as a tedious chore and instead as a key driver of their growth. It's the difference between dreading tax season and excitedly tracking rising profits.

Here's how to make that mental switch:

- **Focus on the Impact:** Every new follower, glowing review, or sale is proof your marketing is working!

- **Gamify It:** Can you beat last month's open rate on your email newsletter? Challenge yourself!

- **Find the Fun:** Do you LOVE making short videos, even if you loathe writing blog posts? Embrace your strengths and make those a priority.

The Exciting Part: No Room for Boredom!

If "same old, same old" makes you yawn, marketing is the cure! There's always:

- **New Skills to Master:** Dive into copywriting, video editing, or even basic design to give you more control over your brand.

- **Trends to Explore:** Could that viral TikTok format be adapted (tastefully) to promote your biz? Experimentation is encouraged!

- **Data as Your Detective Story:** Why did that email subject line crush it? Digging into the "why" is strangely satisfying.

Marketing is an investment in the future of your business. You may not always love every single task, but the results – more customers, increased revenue, the freedom to do work you're passionate about – make the ongoing journey more than worth it!

Resources for Further Learning (blogs, websites, online courses)

"Consider it your personalized toolbox for continuing your marketing mastery quest!"

Warning: The Internet Is a Rabbit Hole of Information

With a few clicks, you could spend the rest of your life consuming free marketing articles and still barely scratch the surface. That's awesome AND overwhelming. Let's curate a list to keep you focused and inspired, not drowning in information overload.

Your Learning Style Matters

How do you absorb knowledge best? This determines what resources will be most helpful:

- **Readers Rejoice:** Blogs and e-books are your jam. You love highlighting key passages and taking notes.

- **Visual Learners:** Video courses, webinars, and infographics make complex concepts click.

- **Doers Delight:** You learn best by DOING, so finding resources with templates, prompts, and step-by-step guides is key.

- **Community Cravers:** You thrive with interaction. Facebook groups or forums let you ask questions and get that dopamine hit when you help others too.

General Marketing Awesomeness (Start Here)

These sites offer a broad overview, perfect for when you need a refresher or want to fill in gaps in your knowledge:

- **HubSpot Blog:** Tons of in-depth articles, especially strong in content marketing and inbound strategies. (https://blog.hubspot.com/marketing)

- **Moz Blog:** Go-to source for all things SEO. They demystify the ever-changing world of pleasing the Google gods. (https://moz.com/blog)

- **Neil Patel:** Opinions vary on his sometimes "bro-y" style, but his content is undeniably actionable, particularly for digital marketing. (https://neilpatel.com/blog/)

- **Social Media Examiner:** As the name suggests, they focus on keeping you up-to-date on platform trends and best practices. (https://www.socialmediaexaminer.com/)

Niche Down for Deeper Dives

Get more specific based on your industry and interests:

- **Creative Freelancers:** The Millo blog and podcast offer a mix of tactical marketing tips and mindset shifts tailored for solopreneurs. (https://millo.co/)

- **E-commerce Mavens:** Shopify's resources are a treasure trove for online store owners, covering everything from product photography to conversion optimization. (https://www.shopify.com/)

- **Local Biz Love:** If your customers are primarily in your area, blogs focused on local SEO and reputation management are golden.

- **Don't Be Afraid of "Boring" Industries:** Often, the most innovative marketing happens in less-sexy niches, precisely because they NEED to stand out.

Online Courses: Level Up at Your Own Pace

Sometimes, you need more structure than random blog surfing provides. Look for courses that:

- **Solve a Specific Problem:** "Build Your First Email List" is more focused than the vague "Marketing 101."

- **Fit Your Budget:** Great freebies exist, along with pricier in-depth options.

- **Match Your Learning Style:** Lots of videos vs. dense PDF workbooks make a huge difference in how well you absorb the info.

- **Taught by People You Admire:** Does their own marketing resonate with you? That's a good sign their methods might work for you too.

Platform-Specific Skill Mastery

- **Facebook Ads Library:** Not technically a course, but seeing what ads your competitors (and successful businesses in unrelated fields) are running is incredibly insightful. (https://www.facebook.com/ads/library/)

- **YouTube Creator Academy:** You don't need to be the next PewDiePie, but their free lessons teach video basics relevant even for business purposes. (https://creatoracademy. youtube.com/)

- **Skillshare:** https://www.skillshare.com/ and Udemy: https://www.udemy.com/: Affordable mini-courses on practically any marketing topic under the sun. Read reviews before diving in, as quality varies.

A Note on "Gurus"

It's easy to get swept up in the promises of overnight marketing success. Be discerning! Look for:

- **Proof of Results:** Case studies, testimonials, and a track record matter more than flashy sales pages.

- **Does Their Style Align with YOURS?:** If you crave data-driven strategies, a hype-filled webinar won't be helpful.

- **Red Flags:** Guarantees of instant riches, bashing other experts, or pushy sales tactics are signs to steer clear.

Your marketing education is a journey, and the resources you find most valuable will evolve over time. Don't be afraid to experiment, and most importantly, have fun along the way!

ADDITIONAL CONSIDERATIONS

Think of it as the "just so you know..." section to round out your marketing knowledge!

The Soft Skills That Make or Break Your Marketing

We've covered tactics and tools, but let's not forget the human side of things. These might not seem directly related to marketing, but trust me, they make a HUGE difference in your success:

- **Empathy:** Truly stepping into your customers' shoes and understanding their struggles is the difference between a bland ad and one that makes them say, "OMG, it's like they read my mind!"

- **Communication:** Whether it's writing clear website copy, answering a tricky customer question, or negotiating with a potential partner... being articulate matters.

- **Resilience:** Not every campaign will be a wild success. The ability to bounce back from flops, analyze what went wrong, and try again is vital.

- **Self-Awareness:** Are you prone to procrastination, a control freak, or a chronic overthinker? Identifying your personal roadblocks helps you work around them or seek help where needed.

How to Develop These Soft Skills

Unlike learning how to use a new software, this stuff is a bit squishier. Here's where to start:

- **Active Listening:** In conversations with customers, truly pay attention. What are their unspoken anxieties and deepest desires beyond the surface-level question?

- **Read Fiction:** Sounds weird, but good novels help you develop empathy by seeing the world through different characters' eyes.

- **Mindset Matters:** Instead of "I'm bad at X," try "I haven't mastered X YET." Growth mindset is everything!

- **Find Your Cheerleaders:** Connecting with other business owners reminds you you're not alone in the struggles, and their wins will inspire you.

Ethical Marketing: Because Success Shouldn't Come at Any Cost

It's tempting in the pursuit of clicks and sales to... *bend* the truth a little. But the internet has a long memory and getting caught in shady practices damages your reputation faster than a bad review. Here's your compass:

- **Transparency is Cool:** Own your pricing, be clear about refund policies, etc. The fewer fine print surprises, the happier customers are long-term.

- **Don't Exploit Fear:** Preying on people's insecurities to sell them quick fixes is gross, even if it sadly works. Build a brand you can be proud of.

- **Give Credit Where Due:** "Borrowing" content without attribution is theft, even if you think no one will notice.

- **Respect Data Privacy:** Those email addresses you worked hard to collect? Treat them with care, and always make it easy to unsubscribe.

Case Study: The Snake Oil Salesman vs. The Trusted Advisor

- **Business #1:** Weight loss product with misleading claims, high-pressure sales tactics, and impossible-to-find refund info. Short-term profits, but a trail of angry customers and potential legal trouble.

- **Business #2:** Fitness coach offering realistic programs, focusing on long-term health. Smaller client base initially, but raving fans bring referrals and the ability to charge premium prices.

Which business model sounds more sustainable (and less likely to bring sleepless nights)?

When to Outsource or Get Help

You can't be an expert in everything. Here's when it's smart to ask for backup:

- **Tasks You Despise:** If editing videos makes you want to hurl, hire it out and focus your energy on what you enjoy.

- **Specialized Skill Sets:** While you can DIY basic logo design, for complex branding or high-stakes projects, a pro is often worth the investment.

- **No Time to Learn:** Could you figure out Google AdWords? Sure. But is that the best use of your CEO hours, or is growing the business more important?

- **Objectivity is Needed:** Sometimes you're too close to your own business to see marketing flaws, and outside perspective is invaluable.

Where to Find Help

- **Freelancer Platforms:** Upwork, Fiverr, etc... word of warning: cheapest isn't always best. Vet carefully by portfolios and reviews.

- **Job Boards:** For local hires or longer-term partnerships. Be clear about expectations to avoid disappointment on both sides.

- **Your Network:** That friend's niece who's amazing at photography? Referrals often work better than cold outreach.

- **Agencies:** Pricier, but ideal for big projects where you need an entire team (copywriter, designer, etc.), not just one freelancer.

It's OKAY to Not Be a Marketing Unicorn

Those entrepreneurs who seem to effortlessly crush it at everything? They have a team behind the scenes, even if they don't broadcast it. Focus on your zone of genius and get strategic about the rest.

The goal of this guide was to empower you, not leave you feeling like you'll never be good enough. Understanding the fundamentals of marketing makes you a savvy business owner capable of making informed decisions, collaborating effectively, and achieving your goals. That's a win worth celebrating!

ACTIONABLE STEPS

From Knowledge to Action: Your Marketing Kickstart

Okay, you've absorbed a ton of information. But the real magic happens when you apply it to YOUR business. Think of this less like homework and more like a choose-your-own-adventure quest!

Step 1: Choose Your Focus

Don't try to tackle EVERYTHING at once. That's a recipe for overwhelm and half-finished projects. Ask yourself:

- **Where's Your Biggest Pain Point?:** No website? Random social posts that get zero engagement? Lack of customer leads? Start where it HURTS the most.

- **What Sparks a Glimmer of Excitement?:** Love the idea of creating videos, but dread writing? Play to your strengths for more sustainable progress.

- **Quick Wins vs. Long-Term Strategy:** Both are necessary! Pick ONE small, actionable thing to improve this week, and ONE foundational task to chip away at.

Step 2: Baby Steps Beat Giant Leaps

Break your chosen focus into ridiculously tiny steps. This prevents that deer-in-headlights feeling:

- **Instead of...** "Create a website"

- **Try...**

  » Tuesday: Buy domain name

  » Wednesday: Research 3 website builders

  » Thursday: Sign up for free trial and poke around

- **Pro-tip:** Timebox these tasks! Thirty minutes of focused effort is more productive than vaguely intending to work on it "sometime" and then procrastinating.

Step 3: Apply What You've Learned

Let's make those marketing concepts REAL for your business:

- **Customer Persona Power-Up:** Don't write another word of marketing copy until you've completed the persona exercise. Knowing WHO you speak to changes everything.

- **Your Ideal "After" Story:** Imagine a satisfied customer raving about your product/service. How did they find you? How did your marketing make them feel along the way? Reverse-engineer to create that experience.

- **Audit Your Existing Stuff:** Does your website, social media, etc. align with your brand values? Is your messaging consistent? Spotting areas for improvement is key.

Examples to Get You Inspired

- **Local Coffee Shop:**

  » Focus: Build community, not just sell lattes.

  » Quick Win: Host a "latte art throwdown" event with prizes.

  » Long Haul: Email newsletter featuring local artists of the month.

- **Freelance Copywriter:**

  » Focus: Stop being a generalist, niche down.

  » Quick Win: Rewrite website headline to target ideal client.

  » Long Haul: Create case study showcasing results for past client in chosen niche.

- **E-commerce Store:**

  » Focus: Improve product descriptions to boost sales.

  » Quick Win: Test two different descriptions for top-selling item, track conversion rate.

  » Long Haul: Add video demos for complex products.

Step 4: Embrace Imperfect Progress

Your first attempt at anything marketing-related will probably be a bit wonky. THAT'S NORMAL! Experts weren't born that way; they iterated (fancy word for trying, learning, and improving).

- **Seek Feedback, Not Perfection:** Show a rough draft to a trusted friend in your target market. Better to fix it now than post something cringey!

- **The "Done is Better Than Perfect" Mantra:** This applies to marketing too! A decent website launched beats endlessly tweaking the font choices.

- **Celebrate the Milestones:** Launched your newsletter? Woo! Ten new Instagram followers? Pat yourself on the back... progress fuels motivation.

Step 5: Visit HeroMarketer.CO

Ready to level up your marketing skills and connect with a community of like-minded professionals? We are developing a website for this book where readers can engage with other readers. The *Zero to Hero Marketer* website is launching soon, packed with articles, resources, and a community for reader interaction. Don't miss out on valuable insights and networking opportunities – visit HeroMarketer.co today to be notified when the site goes live!

This Is Your Marketing Journey

There's no single right path. Experiment, have fun, and tailor what you've learned in this guide to YOUR unique business and personality. You've got this!

REALISTIC EXPECTATIONS

The "Get Rich Quick" Myth vs. Sustainable Growth

L et's be real: if anyone tries to sell you on overnight marketing miracles, run the other way! Building a successful business takes time and consistent effort. Think of marketing as part of the healthy diet for that business, not a fad crash course that leaves you depleted.

The good news is the work you put in compounds over time. It's the difference between shouting your message into the void once versus planting seeds that will blossom for years to come.

Here's why slow and steady wins the marketing race:

- **Trust Takes Time:** Customers don't throw money at strangers. Every positive interaction – a genuinely helpful blog post, a relatable social media update – builds the "know, like, and trust" factor.

- **Search Engines Need Proof:** That awesome new website won't magically rank on the first page of Google overnight. SEO is a long game, but the results are worth it for long-term, consistent traffic.

- **Compounding Results:** The email list you start today might be small. But with nurturing, it yields loyal customers who buy repeatedly and refer their friends.

- **Adaptability is Key:** The marketing landscape WILL change. The foundational skills you gain here make it easier to roll with the punches and spot new opportunities.

Case Study: The Tortoise vs. the Hype-Chasing Hare

- **Business #1:** Gets obsessed with the latest TikTok trend, pours energy into it, then burns out when it doesn't equal instant riches. Their marketing feels scattered and out of touch with who they truly serve.

- **Business #2:** Focuses on timeless principles: solving customer pain points, building an email list, providing value consistently. They may not go viral but attract their DREAM clients and weather any algorithm storms.

Which business would you rather have?

It's a Marathon, Not a Sprint (But a Fun One!)

Yes, there will be moments you want to tear your hair out trying to figure out how to optimize your ad targeting. That's normal! The difference is, you'll now have the tools to work through the challenge instead of giving up altogether.

Learning to market your own business is one of the most empowering things you'll do. Along the way, you might discover:

- **Hidden Talents:** Turns out, you're a pretty decent copywriter once you get the hang of it!

- **The Joy of Connection:** Authentic interactions with customers light you up in a way random "likes" never could.

- **The Confidence Boost:** It's an amazing feeling when your efforts translate into tangible business growth.

Your Marketing Journey is Uniquely Yours

Don't compare yourself to what others seem to achieve. Your path, your pace, and your definition of success will be different. That's the beauty of it!

The concepts in this book are your compass. The more you apply them, the more intuitive marketing will become. There will be wins, stumbles, and plenty of "Aha!" moments along the way.

Embrace the adventure, celebrate the progress, and always remember why you started this journey in the first place – to share your unique gifts with the world. That purpose is your greatest marketing superpower of all!

REMEMBER JOE?

Joe's Transformation: From Hidden Gem to Booked Solid

Remember Joe, the kitchen remodeler whose incredible work was languishing in obscurity? Well, after embracing the strategies we've covered in this book, his business looks radically different.

Here's what's changed:

- **"Word-of-Mouth" 2.0:** Instead of passively hoping for referrals, he now has a system. Happy clients are given gorgeous postcards to share with neighbors, along with an incentive for both parties.

- **Showcase, Not Tell:** His Instagram is filled with stunning before-and-afters, quick video walkthroughs, and client testimonials. Potential homeowners get hooked before even visiting his website.

- **Community Champ:** Partnering with local realtors proved genius. Now, he's THE go-to for pre-listing renovations, and agents actively recommend him.

- **Educate to Empower:** Joe's email newsletter isn't pushy sales pitches. It's packed with design trends, budget-friendly upgrade ideas, and answering FAQs honestly. This builds immense trust.

The biggest shift for Joe wasn't just the calendar full of projects (though that's certainly nice!). It was a change of mindset.

He sees marketing as an extension of his craftsmanship – a way to create a beautiful experience for customers from the moment they discover him until the final countertop is installed.

Success Looks Different for Everyone

Joe isn't quitting his day job to become an influencer. That's not his style. But now, he has the luxury of:

- **Choosing Projects He Loves:** No more settling for picky clients just to pay the bills.

- **Pricing with Confidence:** His reputation and online presence mean he's no longer competing on price alone.

- **Hiring Help:** The increased income means he finally hired an apprentice, freeing him to focus on what he does best.

Marketing transformed Joe's business. But more importantly, it unleashed his entrepreneurial spirit. He's energized, not stressed, and ideas for new offerings based on customer feedback are always buzzing in his head.

Your "After" Story

What might your marketing success story look like?

- The freelance writer who niched down and now commands top rates from dream clients.

- The therapist whose compassionate blog posts lead to a full practice, allowing them to help more people.

- The baker whose online cookie decorating classes create a whole new revenue stream.

It all starts with the willingness to learn and the belief that your work matters. This guide has given you the tools; now it's time to build something amazing!

Marketing is an ever-evolving journey. But the fundamentals you've mastered here will serve you long-term. Embrace the process, celebrate the wins (even the small ones!), and never stop connecting your passion with the people who need it most.

Empowered, Not Overwhelmed

That's the feeling you'll cultivate by the end of this guide. Sure, there will be moments of frustration along the way – that's part of growth! But the difference is, you'll face those challenges with the confidence that you can figure it out.

Marketing is both a skill set AND a mindset. You're further along on this journey than you were a few chapters ago! It's time to celebrate your progress, get out there, and share your amazing work with the world. They're waiting for you!

ABOUT THE AUTHOR

(Who Definitely Wasn't Born Knowing This Stuff)

Nathan Pernia is an entrepreneur and your fellow marketing struggler turned champion. He's not a guru promising instant riches with his "secret sauce." Think of him more like your friend with several seasons in marketing, who's here to cut through the B.S. and share what actually works.

Throughout his career, he's cultivated a deep understanding of marketing by wearing diverse hats: from paste-up newspaper artist and graphic designer to advertising manager, marketing director, and finally, marketing consultant.

Out of countless marketing guides on the shelf, you've chosen this one. This is no coincidence. This book is packed with basic but powerful principles and techniques discussed in this book.

Why He Created This Book

Let's be honest; He's not rolling in the dough, and his client list isn't exactly packed with celebrity names. But hey, that's okay! Because the truth is, he loves marketing. It's like a fascinating puzzle he gets to solve every day, using both his experience and the latest industry tricks to help clients thrive.

The problem? Most marketing advice is either uselessly vague ("Be more brand-y!") or so technical it sounds like gibberish.

That's why he wrote this book. It's his way of giving back and empowering YOU to take charge of your marketing, even if:

- Your last Facebook ad flopped harder than a fish out of water.

- The word "funnel" makes you break into a cold sweat.

- Writing emails feels like pulling teeth (and maybe you'd rather have the dentist do it for real).

This book is like your marketing mentor in a bottle, explaining everything you need to know in a way that's clear, concise, and (dare we say) even fun. It ditches the jargon and dives into the essentials, showing you how to:

- Craft a message that resonates with your audience (without needing a crystal ball)

- Navigate the wild world of social media (without getting lost in the algorithm abyss)

- Turn website visitors into raving fans (without resorting to cheesy sales tactics)

Whether you're a solopreneur, a small business owner, or just someone who wants to understand the marketing magic behind the everyday things you buy, this book is your road map to marketing mastery. So, ditch the confusion and join the hero's journey - your marketing adventure awaits!

Be the Hero Marketer.

Want more? Visit the book website at HeroMarketer.co.

www.ingramcontent.com/pod-product-compliance
Lightning Source LLC
Chambersburg PA
CBHW040926210326
41597CB00030B/5191